Auditing and Related Professional Practice Standards

美国公众公司会计监管委员会审计及相关专业实务准则

（中英对照本 · 第二辑）

北京兆泰投资顾问有限公司 译

法律出版社
LAW PRESS CHINA

图书在版编目(CIP)数据

美国公众公司会计监管委员会审计及相关专业实务准则. 第2辑:汉英对照/北京兆泰投资顾问有限公司编译. —北京:法律出版社,2013.5
ISBN 978-7-5118-4820-8

Ⅰ. ①美… Ⅱ. ①北… Ⅲ. ①审计标准—汇编—美国—汉、英 Ⅳ. ①F239.271.2

中国版本图书馆CIP数据核字(2013)第069028号

美国公众公司会计监管委员会审计及相关专业实务准则(中英对照本·第二辑) | 北京兆泰投资顾问有限公司 译 | 责任编辑 易明群 装帧设计 李 瞻

开本 787毫米×1092毫米 1/16
印张 16.75 **字数** 234千
版本 2013年4月第1版
印次 2013年4月第1次印刷
出版 法律出版社
编辑统筹 学术·对外出版分社
总发行 中国法律图书有限公司
经销 新华书店
印刷 北京中科印刷有限公司
责任印制 陶 松

法律出版社/北京市丰台区莲花池西里7号(100073)
电子邮件/info@lawpress.com.cn
销售热线/010-63939792/9779
网址/www.lawpress.com.cn
咨询电话/010-63939796

中国法律图书有限公司/北京市丰台区莲花池西里7号(100073)
全国各地中法图分、子公司电话:
第一法律书店/010-63939781/9782
西安分公司/029-85388843
重庆公司/023-65382816/2908
上海公司/021-62071010/1636
北京分公司/010-62534456
深圳公司/0755-83072995

书号:ISBN 978-7-5118-4820-8
定价:150.00元
(如有缺页或倒装,中国法律图书有限公司负责退换)

译者的话

《2002年萨班斯－奥克斯利法案》第103条授权美国公众公司会计监督委员会（简称“PCAOB”）为在该委员会登记备案的注册会计师事务所编制和签发公众公司审计报告制定审计准则。PCAOB在成立之初首先将美国注册会计师协会以往发布的审计准则公告作为过渡性审计准则（简称“AU”），并逐步制定正式的PCAOB审计准则（简称“AS”）。我们不难发现，这些审计准则已经在美国上市公司审计中被广泛实施，并受到越来越多其他国家会计监管机构的认可和参考。

我们于2004年5月翻译并由法律出版社出版了《2002年萨班斯－奥克斯利法案》。自2003年12月17日PCAOB发布审计准则第1号以来，截至2013年3月，已经制定了16个审计准则。我们于2007年翻译并由法律出版社出版的第一辑收录了审计准则第1号至第5号，分别是：

- 第1号－在审计报告中援引公众公司会计监管委员会的准则
- 第2号－与财务报表审计合并执行的财务报告内部控制审计（该准则于2007年7月25日被审计准则第5号所替代，因此，第一辑不再收录。）
- 第3号－审计文档
- 第4号－对以前报告的实质性弱点是否依然存在进行报告
- 第5号－与财务报表审计合并执行的财务报告内部控制审计

本书是第二辑，收录了审计准则第6号至第16号，涵盖了审计业务计划阶段和实施阶段的许多重大议题。分别是：

- 第6号－评价财务报表的一致性

- 第 7 号 – 业务质量复核
- 第 8 号 – 审计风险
- 第 9 号 – 审计计划
- 第 10 号 – 审计业务的监督
- 第 11 号 – 在计划和实施审计时对于重要性的考虑
- 第 12 号 – 识别和评估重大错报风险
- 第 13 号 – 审计师对于重大错报风险的应对策略
- 第 14 号 – 评价审计结果
- 第 15 号 – 审计证据
- 第 16 号 – 与审计委员会沟通

对于审计专业词汇的翻译，本书借鉴了国内审计行业的习惯用语，并参考了财政部 2010 年印发的《中国注册会计师执业准则》中使用的相关用词。

在本书出版过程中，法律出版社的责任编辑给予了悉心的指导和无私的帮助，我们在此表示衷心感谢。本书译文虽经反复讨论、修改，其翻译不当之处在所难免，敬请广大读者谅解。

本书的顺利出版是一次成功的团队合作、一次集体智慧的结晶。为其付出辛劳的有：杨峻（CIA、CGA）、郃先宇（CIA、CCSA）、南咏梅（MPA）、刘欣华（CPA）、慕帅和覃帆。

北京兆泰投资顾问有限公司

2013 年 3 月

目　　录

November 15, 2008

2008 年 11 月 15 日

AUDITING AND RELATED PROFESSIONAL PRACTICE STANDARDS
审计及相关专业实务准则

Auditing Standard No. 6 –

审计准则第 6 号 —

Evaluating Consistency of Financial Statements
评价财务报表的一致性

PCAOB

Public Company Accounting Oversight Board

公众公司会计监管委员会

[Effective pursuant to SEC Release No. 34 – 58555, File No. PCAOB – 2008 – 01, September 16, 2008]

[按照 SEC 第 34 – 58555 号公告生效；文件号：PCAOB – 2008 – 01，2008 年 9 月 16 日]

Supersedes AU sec. 420, Consistency of Application of Generally Accepted Accounting Principles and AU sec. 9420, Consistency of Application of Generally Accepted Accounting Principles: Auditing Interpretations of Section 420.

取代过渡性审计准则第 420 条［运用公认会计准则的一致性］和第 9420 条［运用公认会计准则的一致性：第 420 条的审计解释］

Final Rule: PCAOB Release No. 2008 – 001

最终规则：PCAOB 公告第 2008 – 001 号

Table of Contents

目　　录

Paragraph

款　　号

Consistency and the auditor's Report on Financial Statements

一致性和财务报表审计报告

1. This standard establishes requirements and provides direction for the auditor's evaluation of the consistency of the financial statements, including changes to previously issued financial statements, and the effect of that evaluation on the auditor's report on the financial statements.

1. 本准则为审计师评价财务报表（包括对以前发布的财务报表的更正）的一致性，以及该评价对于财务报表审计报告的影响，制定要求并提供指引。

2. To identify consistency matters that might affect the report, the auditor should evaluate whether the comparability of the financial statements between periods has been materially affected by changes in accounting principles or by material adjustments to previously issued financial statements for the relevant periods.

2. 为了识别可能影响审计报告的一致性事项，审计师应当评价各期财务报表的可比性是否受到会计准则变更或者对于以前发布的有关期间的财务报表的重要调整的重大影响。

3. The periods covered in the auditor's evaluation of consistency depend on the periods covered by the auditor's report on the financial statements. When the auditor reports only on the current period, he or she should evaluate whether the current－period financial statements are consistent with those of the preceding period . When the auditor reports

3. 审计师对一致性评价涵盖的期间取决于审计报告涵盖的期间。当审计师仅对当期财务报表出具报告时，应当评价当期财务报表是否与前期的一致。当审计师对两个或两个以上期间出具报告时，如果

on two or more periods, he or she should evaluate consistency between such periods and the consistency of such periods with the period prior thereto if such prior period is presented with the financial statements being reported upon. ①The auditor also should evaluate whether the financial statements for periods described in this paragraph are consistent with previously issued financial statements for the respective periods. ②

该前期与被报告期财务报表一起列报，那么，审计师应当评价这些期间的一致性，以及这些期间与该前期的一致性。审计师还应当评价本款所指期间的财务报表与以前发布的相应期间的财务报表的一致性。

Note: The term "current period" means the most recent year, or period of less than one year, upon which the auditor is reporting.

注："当期"是审计师报告的最近年度或少于一年的期间。

4. The auditor should recognize the following matters relating to the consistency of the company's financial statements in the auditor's report if those matters have a material effect on the financial statements:

4. 如果与公司财务报表一致性有关的下列事项对于财务报表有重大影响，那么，审计师应当在审计报告中予以披露。

a. A change in accounting principle

a. 会计政策变更

b. An adjustment to correct a misstatement in previously issued financial statements. ③

b. 对于已公布财务报表的差错更正

Change in Accounting Principle
会计政策变更

5. A change in accounting principle is a

5. 会计政策变更是从某

change from one generally accepted accounting principle to another generally accepted accounting principle when (1) there are two or more generally accepted accounting principles that apply, or when (2) the accounting principle formerly used is no longer generally accepted. A change in the method of applying an accounting principle also is considered a change in accounting principle. ④

个公认会计准则转为另一个公认会计准则，当（1）适用于两个或两个以上公认会计准则，或（2）原来使用的会计政策已经不再被普遍接受。改变会计政策的使用方法也是会计政策变更。

Note: A change from an accounting principle that is not generally accepted to one that is generally accepted is a correction of a misstatement.

注：从使用不被普遍接受的会计政策改为使用普遍接受的会计政策是错报更正。

6. The auditor should evaluate and report on a change in accounting estimate effected by a change in accounting principle like other changes in accounting principle. ⑤ In addition, the auditor should recognize a change in the reporting entity ⑥by including an explanatory paragraph in the auditor's report, unless the change in reporting entity results from a transaction or event. A change in reporting entity that results from a transaction or event, such as the creation, cessation, or complete or partial purchase or disposition of a subsidiary or other business unit does not require recognition in the auditor's report.

6. 审计师应当如同评价和报告会计政策变更那样评价和报告会计政策变更引起的会计估计变更。另外，除非一项交易或事件导致报告主体变更，否则，审计师应当在审计报告中包含说明段，识别该项变更。一项交易或事件导致的报告主体变更，例如，创设、中止、完成或者部分完成收购或处置子公司或其他类似业务单元，无须在审计报告中披露。

7. The auditor should evaluate a change in accounting principle to determine whether –

7. 审计师应当评价会计政策变更，以便确定：

a. The newly adopted accounting principle is a generally accepted accounting principle,

a. 新采用的会计政策是不是一个公认会计准则，

b. The method of accounting for the effect of the change is in conformity with generally accepted accounting principles,

b. 为该变更的影响而采用的会计方法是否符合公认会计准则，

c. The disclosures related to the accounting change are adequate, ⑦ and

c. 与会计变更有关的披露是否充分，并且

d. The company has justified that the alternative accounting principle is preferable. ⑧

d. 公司能否证明该替代会计政策更好。

8. A change in accounting principle that has a material effect on the financial statements should be recognized in the auditor's report on the audited financial statements. If the auditor concludes that the criteria in paragraph 7 have been met, the auditor should add an explanatory paragraph to the auditor's report, as described in AU sec. 508, Reports on Audited Financial Statements. If those criteria are not met, the auditor should treat this accounting change as a departure from generally accepted accounting principles and address the matter as described in AU sec. 508.

8. 审计师应当在审计报告中披露对于财务报表存在重大影响的会计政策变更。如果审计师认定已经满足第 7 款的标准，那么，审计师应当依照过渡性审计准则第 508 条［报告经审计财务报表］，在审计报告中增加一个说明段。如果不满足那些标准，那么，审计师应当将该会计政策变更视作违背公认会计准则，并依照过渡性审计准则第 508 条进行处理。

Note: If a company's financial statements contain an investment accounted for by the equity method, the auditor's evaluation of consistency should include consideration of the investee. If the investee makes a change in accounting principle that is material to the investing company's financial statements, the auditor should add an explanatory paragraph (following the opinion paragraph) to the auditor's report, as described in AU sec. 508.

注：如果公司财务报表包含某项以权益法核算的投资，审计师的一致性评价应当考虑被投资单位。如果被投资单位的会计政策变更对于投资公司的财务报表是重大的，那么，审计师应当依照过渡性审计准则第 508 条，在审计报告的意见段之后增加一个说明段。

Correction of a Material Misstatement in Previously Issued Financial Statements

对于以前发布的财务报表的重大错报的更正

9. The correction of a material misstatement in previously issued financial statements should be recognized in the auditor's report on the audited financial statements through the addition of an explanatory paragraph, as described in AU sec. 508.

9. 审计师应当依照过渡性审计准则第 508 条的规定，在经审计财务报表的审计报告中增加一个说明段，记载对于以前发布的财务报表的重大错报的更正。

10. The accounting pronouncements generally require certain disclosures relating to restatements to correct misstatements in previously issued financial statements. If the financial statement disclosures are not adequate, the auditor should address the inadequacy of disclosure as described in paragraph 31 of Audi-

10. 会计公告通常要求某些与报表重述有关的披露，用于更正在以前发布的财务报表中的错报。如果财务报表的披露不充分，审计师应当依照审计准则第 14 号［评价审计结果］第

ting Standard No. 14, Evaluating Audit Results, and AU sec. 508.

31 款和过渡性审计准则第 508 条的规定，解决披露的不充分性。

Change in Classification

报表项目重分类

11. Changes in classification in previously issued financial statements do not require recognition in the auditor's report, unless the change represents the correction of a material misstatement or a change in accounting principle. Accordingly, the auditor should evaluate a material change in financial statement classification and the related disclosure to determine whether such a change also is a change in accounting principle or a correction of a material misstatement. For example, certain reclassifications in previously issued financial statements, such as reclassifications of debt from long – term to short – term or reclassifications of cash flows from the operating activities category to the financing activities category, might occur because those items were incorrectly classified in the previously issued financial statements. In such situations, the reclassification also is the correction of a misstatement. If the auditor determines that the reclassification is a change in accounting principle , he or she

11. 除非是重大错报更正或者会计政策变更，否则，对于以前发布的财务报表的重分类不需要在审计报告中识别。因此，审计师应当评价重大的财务报表分类变化及其相关披露，以便确定该变化是否也是会计政策变更或重大错报更正。某些对于以前发布的财务报表的重分类，例如，将长期债务重分类为短期债务，或者，将经营活动现金流量重分类为筹资活动现金流量，可能是由于在以前发布的财务报表中的分类错误导致的。在这些情况下，重分类就是错报更正。如果审计师确定该重分类属于会计政策变更，那么，应当依照第 7、第 8 款和过渡性审计准则第 508 条的

should address the matter as described in paragraphs 7 and 8 and AU sec. 508. If the auditor determines that the reclassification is a correction of a material misstatement in previously issued financial statements, he or she should address the matter as described in paragraphs 9 and 10 and AU sec. 508.

规定处理。如果审计师确定该重分类属于对于以前发布的财务报表的重大错报更正，应当依照本准则第9和10款和过渡性审计准则第508条的规定处理。

① For example, assume that a company presents comparative financial statements covering three years and has a change in auditors. In the first year in which the successor auditor reports, the successor auditor evaluates consistency between the year on which he or she reports and the immediately preceding year. In the second year in which the successor auditor reports, the successor auditor would evaluate consistency between the two years on which he or she reports and between those years and the earliest year presented.

例如，假设某公司披露的可比财务报表包含三个会计年度，并更换了会计师事务所。在后任审计师第一年的审计报告中，后任审计师评价该年度与上一年度的一致性。在第二年的审计报告中，后任审计师应当评价由其审计的这两年的一致性，以及这些年度与最早披露年度的一致性。

② When a company uses retrospective application, as defined in Statement of Financial Accounting Standards No. 154, Accounting Changes and Error Corrections ("SFAS No. 154"), to account for a change in accounting principle, the financial statements presented generally will be consistent. However, the previous years' financial statements presented with the current year's financial statements will reflect the change in accounting principle and, therefore, will appear different from those previous years' financial statements on which the auditor previously reported. This standard clarifies that the auditor's evaluation of consistency should encompass previously issued financial statements for the relevant periods.

当某公司采用美国财务会计准则公告第154号［会计变更和差错更正］（"SFAS No. 154"）规定的追溯调整法核算会计政策变更，列报的财务报表通常是一致的。但是，与本年财务报表一同列报的以前年度财务报表会反映该会计政策变更，也就会看起来不同于审计师以前报告的以前年度财务报表。本准则明确要求审计师的一致性评价应当涵盖相关期间以前发布的财务报表。

③ [Footnote deleted, effective for audits of fiscal years beginning on or after December 15, 2010. See PCAOB Release No. 2010-004.]

由于本脚注已不适用于2010年12月15日（含）开始的会计年度审计，因此删除。参见PCAOB第2010-004号公告。

④ See SFAS No. 154, paragraph 2c.

参见 SFAS 第 154 号第 2c 款。

⑤ SFAS No. 154, paragraph 2e, defines a "change in accounting estimate effected by a change in accounting principle" as "a change in accounting estimate that is inseparable from the effect of a related change in accounting principle."

SFAS 第 154 号第 2e 款将“会计政策变更引起的会计估计变更”定义为“与会计政策变更不可分的会计估计变更”。

⑥ "Change in reporting entity" is a change that results in financial statements that, in effect, are those of a different reporting entity. See SFAS No. 154, paragraph 2f.

“报告主体变更”实际上是由不同的报告主体编报财务报表而产生的变更。

⑦ Newly issued accounting pronouncements usually set forth the method of accounting for the effects of a change in accounting principle and the related disclosures. SFAS No. 154 sets forth the method of accounting for the change and the related disclosures when there are no specific requirements in the new accounting pronouncement.

新发布的会计公告通常详尽地解释某项会计准则变更及其相关披露的会计方法。若某项新的会计公告没有具体的要求，SFAS 第 154 号详尽地解释了对于变更及其相关披露的会计方法。

⑧ The issuance of an accounting pronouncement that requires use of a new accounting principle, interprets an existing principle, expresses a preference for an accounting principle, or rejects a specific principle is sufficient justification for a change in accounting principle, as long as the change in accounting principle is made in accordance with the hierarchy of generally accepted accounting principles. See SFAS No. 154, paragraph 14.

只要会计政策变更符合公认会计准则的层级制度，那么，要求采用某条新会计准则、阐释某条现行会计准则、表达优先使用某条会计准则或者拒绝使用某条特定会计准则的会计公告就是会计政策变更的充分依据。参见 SFAS 第 154 号第 14 款。

December 15, 2009
2009 年 12 月 15 日

AUDITING AND RELATED PROFESSIONAL PRACTICE STANDARDS
审计及相关专业实务准则

Auditing Standard No. 7 –
审计准则第 7 号 —

Engagement Quality Review
业务质量复核

PCAOB

Public Company Accounting Oversight Board
公众公司会计监管委员会

[Effective pursuant to SEC Release No. 34 – 61363, File No. PCAOB – 2009 – 02, January 15, 2010]
[按照 SEC 第 34 – 61363 号公告生效；文件号：PCAOB – 2009 – 02，2010 年 1 月 15 日]

Supersedes SECPS Requirements of Membership § 1000.08 (f).
取代 SEC Practice Section 会员要求第 1000.08 (f) 条

Final Rule: PCAOB Release 2009 – 004
最终规则：PCAOB 公告第 2009 – 004 号

Table of Contents

目　　录

Paragraph

款　　号

Applicability of Standard
准则的适用性

1. An engagement quality review and concurring approval of issuance are required for each audit engagement and for each engagement to review interim financial information conducted pursuant to the standards of the Public Company Accounting Oversight Board ("PCAOB").

1. 根据美国公众公司会计监督委员会（"PCAOB"）的准则实施的每一项审计业务和中期财务资料审阅业务均须进行业务质量复核以及联名批准。

Objective
目　标

2. The objective of the engagement quality reviewer is to perform an evaluation of the significant judgments made by the engagement team and the related conclusions reached in forming the overall conclusion on the engagement and in preparing the engagement report, if a report is to be issued, in order to determine whether to provide concurring approval of issuance. ①

2. 业务质量复核人员的目标是评价业务团队为了对业务的总体情况做出结论并（如果需要的话）出具报告而做出的重大判断及其相关结论，以便决定是否联名批准发布报告。

Qualifications of an Engagement Quality Reviewer
业务质量复核人员的资质

3. The engagement quality reviewer must be an associated person of a registered public

3. 业务质量复核人员必须是在册会计师事务所的

accounting firm. An engagement quality reviewer from the firm that issues the engagement report (or communicates an engagement conclusion, if no report is issued) must be a partner or another individual in an equivalent position. The engagement quality reviewer may also be an individual from outside the firm. ②

在职人员。发布业务报告（或者，不发布报告而是表达业务结论）的事务所的业务质量复核人员必须是合伙人或者同等职位的其他人员。业务质量复核人员也可以是事务所之外的人员。

4. As described below, an engagement quality reviewer must have competence, independence, integrity, and objectivity.

4. 如下所述，业务质量复核人员必须胜任、独立、诚信和客观。

Note: The firm's quality control policies and procedures should include provisions to provide the firm with reasonable assurance that the engagement quality reviewer has sufficient competence, independence, integrity, and objectivity to perform the engagement quality review in accordance with the standards of the PCAOB.

注：事务所的质量控制政策和程序应当包含有关规定，为事务所合理保证业务质量复核人员胜任、独立、诚信和客观，使其遵照 PCAOB 的准则实施业务质量复核。

Competence

胜任

5. The engagement quality reviewer must possess the level of knowledge and competence related to accounting, auditing, and financial reporting required to serve as the engagement partner on the engagement under

5. 业务质量复核人员必须具备会计、审计和财务报告的相关知识和胜任能力水平，以便作为被复核业务的业务合伙人。

review. ③

Independence, Integrity, and Objectivity
独立、诚信和客观

6. The engagement quality reviewer must be independent of the company, perform the engagement quality review with integrity, and maintain objectivity in performing the review.

6. 业务质量复核人员必须独立于审计客户，诚信地实施业务质量复核，在复核业务过程中保持客观。

Note: The reviewer may use assistants in performing the engagement quality review. Personnel assisting the engagement quality reviewer also must be independent, perform the assigned procedures with integrity, and maintain objectivity in performing the review.

注：复核人员在实施业务质量复核时可以使用助理人员。协助业务质量复核人员的助理人员也必须独立，诚信地实施被分派的程序，并且在复核过程中保持客观。

7. To maintain objectivity, the engagement quality reviewer and others who assist the reviewer should not make decisions on behalf of the engagement team or assume any of the responsibilities of the engagement team. The engagement partner remains responsible for the engagement and its performance, notwithstanding the involvement of the engagement quality reviewer and others who assist the reviewer.

7. 为了保持客观，业务质量复核人员和助理人员不应当替业务团队做决定或履行业务团队的任何职责。不论是否存在业务质量复核人员和助理人员，业务合伙人仍应对该业务及其实施承担责任。

8. The person who served as the engagement partner during either of the two audits preceding the audit subject to the engagement quality review may not be the engagement quality reviewer. Registered firms that qualify for the exemption under Rule 2 – 01 (c) (6) (ii) of Regulation S – X, 17 C. F. R. § 210. 2 – 01 (c) (6) (ii), are exempt from the requirement in this paragraph.

8. 在接受业务质量复核的某审计业务的前两个审计期间中的任一期间担任业务合伙人的人员不得作为该业务的业务质量复核人员。满足 Rule 2 – 01 (c) (6) (ii) of Regulation S – X, 17 C. F. R. § 210. 2 – 01 (c) (6) (ii) 要求的在册事务所获得本款规定的豁免。

Engagement Quality Review for an Audit
审计业务质量复核

Engagement Quality Review Process
业务质量复核程序

9. In an audit engagement, the engagement quality reviewer should evaluate the significant judgments made by the engagement team and the related conclusions reached in forming the overall conclusion on the engagement and in preparing the engagement report. To evaluate such judgments and conclusions, the engagement quality reviewer should, to the extent necessary to satisfy the requirements of paragraphs 10 and 11: (1) hold discussions with the engagement partner

9. 对于审计业务，业务质量复核人员应当评价业务团队为了对业务的总体情况做出结论并编制业务报告而做出的重大判断及其相关结论。为了评价这些判断和结论，业务质量复核人员应当（1）与业务合伙人和业务团队的其他成员进行讨论，并且（2）复核文档，以便满足

and other members of the engagement team, and (2) review documentation.

第 10 和 11 款的要求。

10. In an audit, the engagement quality reviewer should:

10. 对于审计业务，业务质量复核人员应当：

a. Evaluate the significant judgments that relate to engagement planning, including -

a. 评价与业务计划有关的重大判断，包括

• The consideration of the firm's recent engagement experience with the company and risks identified in connection with the firm's client acceptance and retention process,

• 考虑事务所在该公司的近期业务经验，以及在接纳和保留客户过程中识别的风险，

• The consideration of the company's business, recent significant activities, and related financial reporting issues and risks, and

• 该公司的经营、近期重大业务活动和相关财务报告事项和风险，以及

• The judgments made about materiality and the effect of those judgments on the engagement strategy.

• 对于重要性的判断及其对于业务策略的影响。

b. Evaluate the engagement team's assessment of, and audit responses to -

b. 评价业务团队对以下事项的评估和审计应对策略—

• Significant risks identified by the engagement team, including fraud risks, and

• 审计团队识别的重大风险（包括舞弊风险），和

• Other significant risks identified by the en-

• 业务质量复核人员按照

gagement quality reviewer through performance of the procedures required by this standard.

本准则的要求而执行的程序所识别的其他重大风险。

Note: A significant risk is a risk of material misstatement that requires special audit consideration.

重大风险是实质性错报的风险，需要受到特别的审计考虑。

c. Evaluate the significant judgments made about (1) the materiality and disposition of corrected and uncorrected identified misstatements and (2) the severity and disposition of identified control deficiencies.

c. 评价以下重大判断，（1）重要性以及已纠正和未纠正的已识别重大错报的处理结果，和（2）已识别控制缺陷的严重性和处理结果。

d. Review the engagement team's evaluation of the firm's independence in relation to the engagement.

d. 复核业务团队有关本事务所在该项业务中的独立性的评价。

e. Review the engagement completion document [4] and confirm with the engagement partner that there are no significant unresolved matters.

e. 复核已完成的业务文档，并且与业务合伙人确认没有未解决事项。

f. Review the financial statements, management's report on internal control, and the related engagement report.

f. 复核财务报表、管理层的内部控制报告和相关业务报告。

g. Read other information in documents containing the financial statements to be filed

g. 阅读将向美国证券交易委员会（"SEC"）申报

with the Securities and Exchange Commission ("SEC") ⑤ and evaluate whether the engagement team has taken appropriate action with respect to any material inconsistencies with the financial statements or material misstatements of fact of which the engagement quality reviewer is aware.

的包含经审计财务报表的文件中的其他资料，并且评价业务团队针对业务质量复核人员已知的任何与财务报表的重大不一致或者事实的重大错报是否采取适当行动。

h. Based on the procedures required by this standard, evaluate whether appropriate consultations have taken place on difficult or contentious matters. Review the documentation, including conclusions, of such consultations.

h. 基于本准则所要求的程序，评价是否针对难题和争议事项进行了适当的磋商。复核包括这些磋商在内的文档。

i. Based on the procedures required by this standard, evaluate whether appropriate matters have been communicated, or identified for communication, to the audit committee, management, and other parties, such as regulatory bodies.

i. 基于本准则所要求的程序，评价是否已经与审计委员会、管理层和其他方面，例如，监管部门，沟通了适当事项，或者已经识别出来，以便沟通。

Evaluation of Engagement Documentation

业务文档的评价

11. In an audit, the engagement quality reviewer should evaluate whether the engagement documentation that he or she reviewed when performing the procedures required by paragraph 10 –

11. 对于审计业务，业务质量复核人员按照第 10 款实施复核程序时应当评价业务文档是否

a. Indicates that the engagement team responded appropriately to significant risks, and

a. 表明业务团队适当地应对了重大风险，并且

b. Supports the conclusions reached by the engagement team with respect to the matters reviewed.

b. 支持业务团队针对被复核事项所做的结论。

Concurring Approval of Issuance
发布报告的联名批准

12. In an audit, the engagement quality reviewer may provide concurring approval of issuance only if, after performing with due professional care [6] the review required by this standard, he or she is not aware of a significant engagement deficiency.

12. 对于审计业务，业务质量复核人员只有以职业审慎实施了本准则要求的复核，在未发现任何重大业务缺陷之后，才可以联名批准。

Note: A significant engagement deficiency in an audit exists when (1) the engagement team failed to obtain sufficient appropriate evidence in accordance with the standards of the PCAOB, (2) the engagement team reached an inappropriate overall conclusion on the subject matter of the engagement, (3) the engagement report is not appropriate in the circumstances, or (4) the firm is not independent of its client.

注：以下情形表明审计业务存在重大业务缺陷，（1）业务团队没有遵照 PCAOB 准则的要求取得充分适当的证据，（2）业务团队在业务的鉴证事项上得出不适当的总体结论，（3）业务报告是不适当的，或者（4）事务所不独立于该审计客户。

13. In an audit, the firm may grant permission to the client to use the engagement report only

13. 对于审计业务，事务所只有在业务质量复核人

after the engagement quality reviewer provides concurring approval of issuance. ⑦

员联名批准公布之后才可以允许客户使用业务报告。

Engagement Quality Review for a Review of Interim Financial Information

中期财务资料审阅业务质量复核

Engagement Quality Review Process

业务质量复核程序

14. In an engagement to review interim financial information, the engagement quality reviewer should evaluate the significant judgments made by the engagement team and the related conclusions reached in forming the overall conclusion on the engagement and in preparing the engagement report, if a report is to be issued. To evaluate such judgments and conclusions, the engagement quality reviewer should, to the extent necessary to satisfy the requirements of paragraphs 15 and 16: (1) hold discussions with the engagement partner and other members of the engagement team, and (2) review documentation.

14. 对于中期财务资料审阅业务，业务质量复核人员应当评价业务团队为了对业务的总体情况做出结论并（如果签发报告的话）编制业务报告而做出的重大判断及其相关结论。为了评价这些判断和结论，（1）与业务合伙人和业务团队的其他成员进行讨论，并且（2）复核文档，以便满足第 15 和 16 款的要求。

15. In a review of interim financial information, the engagement quality reviewer

15. 对于中期财务资料审阅业务，业务质量复核人

should:

员应当：

a. Evaluate the significant judgments that relate to engagement planning, including the consideration of -

a. 评价与业务计划有关的重大判断，包括考虑：

• The firm's recent engagement experience with the company and risks identified in connection with the firm's client acceptance and retention process,

• 事务所在该公司的近期业务经验，以及在接纳和保留客户过程中识别的风险，

• The company's business, recent significant activities, and related financial reporting issues and risks, and

• 该公司的经营、近期重大业务活动和相关财务报告事项和风险，以及

• The nature of identified risks of material misstatement due to fraud.

• 识别的与舞弊有关的重大错报风险的性质。

b. Evaluate the significant judgments made about (1) the materiality and disposition of corrected and uncorrected identified misstatements and (2) any material modifications that should be made to the disclosures about changes in internal control over financial reporting.

b. 评价以下重大判断，(1) 重要性以及已纠正和未纠正的已识别重大错报的处理结果，和 (2) 对于财务报告内部控制的变化所做披露应当做出的重大修改。

c. Perform the procedures described in paragraphs 10. d and 10. e.

c. 实施第 10. d 和 10. e 款要求的程序。

d. Review the interim financial information

d. 复核所有披露期间和紧

for all periods presented and for the immediately preceding interim period, management's disclosure for the period under review, if any, about changes in internal control over financial reporting, and the related engagement report, if a report is to be issued.

邻中期之前期间的中期财务资料、当前复核期间的管理层对于财务报告内部控制的变化所做的披露(如果有的话),以及相关的业务报告(如果签发的话)。

e. Read other information in documents containing interim financial information to be filed with the SEC ⑧ and evaluate whether the engagement team has taken appropriate action with respect to material inconsistencies with the interim financial information or material misstatements of fact of which the engagement quality reviewer is aware.

e. 阅读将向 SEC 申报的包含中期财务资料的文件中的其他资料，并且评价业务团队针对业务质量复核人员已知的任何与中期财务资料的重大不一致或者事实的重大错报是否采取适当行动。

f. Perform the procedures in paragraphs 10. h and 10. i

f. 实施第 10. h 和 10. i 款的程序。

Evaluation of Engagement Documentation

评价业务文档

16. In a review of interim financial information, the engagement quality reviewer should evaluate whether the engagement documentation that he or she reviewed when performing the procedures required by paragraph 15 supports the conclusions reached by the engagement team with respect to the matters reviewed.

16. 对于中期财务资料审阅业务，业务质量复核人员按照第 15 款实施复核程序时，应当评价业务文档是否支持业务团队针对被复核事项所做的结论。

Concurring Approval of Issuance
发布报告的联名批准

17. In a review of interim financial information, the engagement quality reviewer may provide concurring approval of issuance only if, after performing with due professional care the review required by this standard, he or she is not aware of a significant engagement deficiency.

17. 对于中期财务资料审阅业务，业务质量复核人员只有以职业审慎实施了本准则要求的复核，没有发现任何重大业务缺陷，才可以联名批准。

Note: A significant engagement deficiency in a review of interim financial information exists when (1) the engagement team failed to perform interim review procedures necessary in the circumstances of the engagement, (2) the engagement team reached an inappropriate overall conclusion on the subject matter of the engagement, (3) the engagement report is not appropriate in the circumstances, or (4) the firm is not independent of its client.

注：以下情形表明中期财务资料审阅业务存在重大业务缺陷，（1）业务团队没有根据业务情况实施必要的中期审阅程序，（2）业务团队在业务的鉴证事项上得出不适当的总体结论，（3）业务报告是不适当的，或者（4）事务所不独立于该客户。

18. In a review of interim financial information, the firm may grant permission to the client to use the engagement report (or communicate an engagement conclusion to its client, if no report is issued) only after the engagement quality reviewer provides concurring approval of issuance.

18. 对于中期财务资料审阅业务，事务所只有在业务质量复核人员联名批准公布之后才可以允许客户使用业务报告。

Documentation of an Engagement Quality Review
业务质量复核的文档

19. Documentation of an engagement quality review should contain sufficient information to enable an experienced auditor, having no previous connection with the engagement, to understand the procedures performed by the engagement quality reviewer, and others who assisted the reviewer, to comply with the provisions of this standard, including information that identifies:

19. 业务质量复核的文档应当包含充分的资料，使得原先没有接触过该业务的熟练的审计人员能够了解业务质量复核人员和其他助理人员按照本准则实施的程序，包括识别以下各项的资料：

a. The engagement quality reviewer, and others who assisted the reviewer,

a. 业务质量复核人员和其他助理人员，

b. The documents reviewed by the engagement quality reviewer, and others who assisted the reviewer,

b. 业务质量复核人员和其他助理人员复核的文档，

c. The date the engagement quality reviewer provided concurring approval of issuance or, if no concurring approval of issuance was provided, the reasons for not providing the approval.

c. 业务质量复核人员签署联名批准的日期，或者，没有签署联名批准的理由。

20. Documentation of an engagement quality review should be included in the engagement documentation.

20. 业务质量复核的文档应当包含在该业务文档中。

21. The requirements related to retention of

21. PCAOB 审计准则第3

and subsequent changes to audit documentation in PCAOB Auditing Standard No. 3, Audit Documentation, apply with respect to the documentation of the engagement quality review.

号［审计文档］有关保管和变更审计文档的要求适用于业务质量复核文档。

---

① In the context of an audit, "engagement report" refers to the audit report (or reports if, in an integrated audit, the auditor issues separate reports on the financial statements and internal control over financial reporting). In the context of an engagement to review interim financial information, the term refers to the report on interim financial information. An engagement report might not be issued in connection with a review of interim financial information. See paragraph .03 of AU section ("sec.") 722, Interim Financial Information.

对于审计而言，"业务报告"是指审计报告即审计师分别发布财务报表审计报告和财务报告内部控制审计报告。对于中期财务资料审阅而言，业务报告是指中期业务资料审阅报告。审阅中期业务资料也可以不发布业务报告。参见过渡性审计准则第 722 条［中期财务资料］第.03 款。

② An outside reviewer who is not already associated with a registered public accounting firm would become associated with the firm issuing the report if he or she (rather than, or in addition to, his or her firm or other employer): (1) receives compensation from the firm issuing the report for performing the review or (2) performs the review as agent for the firm issuing the report. See PCAOB Rule 1001 (p) (i) for the definition of an associated person of a registered public accounting firm.

任何未在在册会计师事务所任职的外部复核人员一旦（1）收取发布报告的该所为复核所支付的报酬，或者（2）作为发布报告的该所雇佣的代理人实施了复核，即被看作是该所的在职人员。关于在册会计师事务所在职人员的定义请参见 PCAOB 规则第 1001（p）（i）条。

③ The term "engagement partner" has the same meaning as the "practitioner – in – charge of an engagement" in PCAOB interim quality control standard QC sec. 40, The Personnel Management Element of a Firm's System of Quality Control – Competencies Required by a Practitioner – in – Charge of an Attest Engagement. QC sec. 40 describes the competencies required of a practitioner – in – charge of an attest engagement.

"业务合伙人"与 PCAOB 过渡性质量控制准则第 40 条（QC sec. 40）［事务所质量控制体系的人员管理要素 - 负责鉴证业务的从业人员所需胜任能力］所指的"负责鉴证业务的从业人员"具有相同含义。QC sec. 40 规定了负责鉴证业务的从业人员所需的胜任能力。

④ Paragraph 13 of PCAOB Auditing Standard No. 3, Audit Documentation, requires the auditor to identify all significant findings or issues in an engagement completion document.

PCAOB 审计准则第 3 号［审计文档］第 13 款要求审计师在业务完成 文档中识别所有重大发现和事项。

⑤ See paragraphs .04 –.06 of AU sec. 550, Other Information in Documents Containing Audited Financial Statements; AU sec. 711, Filings Under Federal Securities Statutes.

参见过渡性审计准则第 550 条［包含经审计财务报表的文件中的其他资料］第 .04 至 .06 款；过渡性审计准则第 711 条［遵照联邦证券法律申报］。

⑥ See AU sec. 230, Due Professional Care in the Performance of Work.

参见过渡性审计准则第 230 条［业务实施中的职业审慎］

⑦ Concurring approval of issuance by the engagement quality reviewer also is required when reissuance of an engagement report requires the auditor to update his or her procedures for subsequent events. In that case, the engagement quality reviewer should update the engagement quality review by addressing those matters related to the subsequent events procedures.

当重新公布业务报告需要审计师为期后事项更新其程序时，也要求业务质量复核人员联名批准公布报告。此时，业务质量复核人员应当针对与期后事项程序有关的事项更新其业务质量复核。

⑧ See AU sec. 722.18f; AU sec. 711.

参见过渡性审计准则第 722 条第 18f 款；过渡性审计准则第 711 条。

December 15, 2010
2010 年 12 月 15 日

AUDITING AND RELATED PROFESSIONAL PRACTICE STANDARDS
审计及相关专业实务准则

Auditing Standard No. 8 –
审计准则第 8 号 —

Audit Risk
审计风险

PCAOB

Public Company Accounting Oversight Board
公众公司会计监管委员会

[Effective pursuant to SEC Release No. 34 – 63606, File No. PCAOB – 2010 – 01, December 23, 2010]
[按照 SEC 第 34 – 63606 号公告生效；文件号：PCAOB – 2010 – 01，2012 年 12 月 23 日]

Final Rule: PCAOB Release No. 2010 – 004
最终规则：PCAOB 公告第 2010 – 004 号

Table of Contents

目　　录

Paragraph

款　　号

Introduction
引　　言

1. This standard discusses the auditor's consideration of audit risk in an audit of financial statements as part of an integrated audit [①] or an audit of financial statements only.

1. 本准则讨论审计师在作为整合审计的一部分的财务报表审计或者单独的财务报表审计中对于风险的考虑。

Objective
目　　标

2. The objective of the auditor is to conduct the audit of financial statements in a manner that reduces audit risk to an appropriately low level.

2. 审计师的目标是将审计风险降低到适当的低水平。

Audit Risk
审计风险

3. To form an appropriate basis for expressing an opinion on the financial statements, the auditor must plan and perform the audit to obtain reasonable assurance about whether the financial statements are free of material misstatement[②] due to error or fraud. Reasonable assurance[③] is obtained by reducing audit risk to an appropriately low level through applying due professional care, including obtaining

3. 为了形成发表财务报表审计意见的适当基础，审计师必须计划和实施审计，针对财务报表是否没有错误或舞弊造成的重大错报，获得合理保证。合理保证是通过运用职业审慎，包括获取充分适当的审计证据，将审计风险降

sufficient appropriate audit evidence.

低到适当的低水平。

4. In an audit of financial statements, audit risk is the risk that the auditor expresses an inappropriate audit opinion when the financial statements are materially misstated, i. e. , the financial statements are not presented fairly in conformity with the applicable financial reporting framework. Audit risk is a function of the risk of material misstatement and detection risk.

4. 对于财务报表审计业务，审计风险是财务报表存在重大错报时，例如，财务报表没有按照适当的财务报告框架披露，审计师发表了不适当的审计意见。审计风险是重大错报风险和检查风险的函数。

Note: The auditor should look to the requirements of the Securities and Exchange Commission for the company under audit with respect to the accounting principles applicable to that company.

注：审计师应当留意美国证券交易委员会关于该被审计公司所适用的会计政策的有关要求。

Risk of Material Misstatement
重大错报风险

5. The risk of material misstatement refers to the risk that the financial statements are materially misstated. Auditing Standard No. 12, Identifying and Assessing Risks of Material Misstatement , indicates that the auditor should assess the risks of material misstatement at two levels: (1) at the financial statement level and (2) at the assertion[4] level. [5]

5. 重大错报风险是指财务报表被重大错报的风险。审计准则第 12 号［识别和评估重大错报风险］指出，审计师应当在两个层次上评估重大错报风险：（1）财务报表层次，和（2）认定层次。

6. Risks of material misstatement at the financial statement level relate pervasively to the financial statements as a whole and potentially affect many assertions. Risks of material misstatement at the financial statement level may be especially relevant to the auditor's consideration of the risk of material misstatement due to fraud. For example, an ineffective control environment, a lack of sufficient capital to continue operations, and declining conditions affecting the company's industry might create pressures or opportunities for management to manipulate the financial statements, leading to higher risk of material misstatement.

6. 财务报表层次的重大错报风险广泛地与财务报表整体相关，而且可能影响许多认定。财务报表层次的重大错报风险也许尤其与审计师考虑的舞弊造成的重大错报风险相关。例如，无效的控制环境、缺乏持续运营所需的充足资本、波及该公司所处行业的衰退可能迫使或诱使管理层操纵财务报表，导致更高的重大错报风险。

7. Risk of material misstatement at the assertion level consists of the following components:

7. 认定层次重大错报风险由以下部分组成：

a. Inherent risk, which refers to the susceptibility of an assertion to a misstatement, due to error or fraud, that could be material, individually or in combination with other misstatements, before consideration of any related controls.

a. 固有风险，即某个认定对于错误或舞弊造成的错报而言的脆弱性，而在考虑任何相关控制之前，该错报单独或与其他错报合并可能是重大的。

b. Control risk, which is the risk that a misstatement due to error or fraud that could occur in an assertion and that could be materi-

b. 控制风险，即该公司的内部控制不能防止或及时发现错误或舞弊造成的

al, individually or in combination with other misstatements, will not be prevented or detected on a timely basis by the company's internal control. Control risk is a function of the effectiveness of the design and operation of internal control.

错报，而在考虑任何相关控制之前，该错报单独或与其他错报合并可能是重大的。控制风险是内部控制的设计有效性和运行有效性的函数。

8. Inherent risk and control risk are related to the company, its environment, and its internal control, and the auditor assesses those risks based on evidence he or she obtains. The auditor assesses inherent risk using information obtained from performing risk assessment procedures and considering the characteristics of the accounts and disclosures in the financial statements. ⑥ The auditor assesses control risk using evidence obtained from tests of controls (if the auditor plans to rely on those controls to assess control risk at less than maximum) and from other sources. ⑦

8. 固有风险和控制风险与公司、所处环境及其内部控制有关，审计师根据所获证据评估这些风险。审计师利用在实施风险评估程序以及考虑财务报表账户和披露的特点过程中所获得的证据评估这些风险。审计师利用在控制测试（如果审计师计划依赖这些控制，从而将控制风险评估为低于最大水平）和其他渠道所获得的证据评估控制风险。

Detection Risk
检查风险

9. In an audit of financial statements, detection risk is the risk that the procedures performed by the auditor will not detect a misstatement that exists and that could be material, individually or in combination with oth-

9. 对于财务报表审计业务，检查风险是审计师实施的程序没有发现错报，而该错报单独或与其他错报合并可能是重大的。检

er misstatements. Detection risk is affected by (1) the effectiveness of the substantive procedures and (2) their application by the auditor, i. e. , whether the procedures were performed with due professional care.

查风险受到（1）实质性程序的有效性和（2）审计师对其运用的影响，例如，是否以职业审慎实施了程序。

10. The auditor uses the assessed risk of material misstatement to determine the appropriate level of detection risk for a financial statement assertion. The higher the risk of material misstatement, the lower the level of detection risk needs to be in order to reduce audit risk to an appropriately low level.

10. 审计师利用重大错报评定风险确定适当的财务报表认定的检查风险水平。较高的重大错报风险需要较低的检查风险水平，从而将审计风险降低到适当的低水平。

11. The auditor reduces the level of detection risk through the nature, timing, and extent of the substantive procedures performed. As the appropriate level of detection risk decreases, the evidence from substantive procedures that the auditor should obtain increases. ⑧

11. 审计师通过实施实质性程序的性质、时间和范围降低检查风险的水平。当适当的检查风险水平降低时，审计师从实质性程序获得的证据应当增加。

① When the auditor is performing an integrated audit of financial statements and internal control over financial reporting, the requirements in Auditing Standard No. 5, An Audit of Internal Control Over Financial Reporting That Is Integrated with An Audit of Financial Statements, also apply. However, the risks of material misstatement of the financial statements are the same for both the audit of financial statements and the audit of internal control over financial reporting.

审计准则第5号［与财务报表审计合并执行的财务报告内部控制审计］也适用于审计师实施的财务报表和财务报告内部控制整合审计。但是，财务报表审计和财务报告内部控制审计两者的财务报表重大错报风险是相同的。

② Misstatement is defined in Appendix A of Auditing Standard No. 14, Evaluating Audit Results.

错报的定义请见审计准则第 14 号［评价审计结果］的附录 A。

③ See AU sec. 110, Responsibilities and Functions of the Independent Auditor, and paragraph .10 of AU sec. 230, Due Professional Care in the Performance of Work, for a further discussion of reasonable assurance.

有关合理保证的深入讨论请参见过渡性审计准则第 110 条［独立审计师的责任和作用］和过渡性审计准则第 230 条［业务实施中的职业审慎］第 .10 款。

④ See Auditing Standard No. 15, Audit Evidence, for a description of financial statement assertions.

有关财务报表认定的描述请参见审计准则第 15 号［审计证据］

⑤ Paragraph 59 of Auditing Standard No. 12.

审计准则第 12 号第 59 款。

⑥ Paragraph 59. a. of Auditing Standard No. 12.

审计准则第 12 号第 59. a 款。

⑦ Paragraphs 32 – 34 of Auditing Standard No. 13, The auditor's Responses to the Risks of Material Misstatement.

审计准则第 13 号［审计师对于重大错报风险的应对策略］第 32 至 34 款。

⑧ Paragraph 37 of Auditing Standard No. 13.

审计准则第 13 号第 37 款。

December 15, 2010
2010 年 12 月 15 日

AUDITING AND RELATED PROFESSIONAL PRACTICE STANDARDS
审计及相关专业实务准则

Auditing Standard No. 9 –
审计准则第 9 号 —

Audit Planning
审计计划

PCAOB

Public Company Accounting Oversight Board
公众公司会计监管委员会

[Effective pursuant to SEC Release No. 34 – 63606, File No. PCAOB – 2010 – 01, December 23, 2010]
[按照 SEC 第 34 – 63606 号公告生效；文件号：PCAOB – 2010 – 01，2012 年 12 月 23 日]

Final Rule: PCAOB Release No. 2010 – 004
最终规则：PCAOB 公告第 2010 – 004 号

Table of Contents

目　　录

Paragraph

款　　号

Introduction
引　言

1. This standard establishes requirements regarding planning an audit.

1. 本准则为审计计划工作制定要求。

Objective
目　标

2. The objective of the auditor is to plan the audit so that the audit is conducted effectively.

2. 审计师的目标是制定审计计划，从而有效地执行审计。

Responsibility of the Engagement Partner for Planning
业务合伙人对于计划的责任

3. **The engagement partner**① is responsible for the engagement and its performance . Accordingly, the engagement partner is responsible for planning the audit and may seek assistance from appropriate engagement team members in fulfilling this responsibility. Engagement team members who assist the engagement partner with audit planning also should comply with the relevant requirements in this standard.

3. 业务合伙人对审计业务及其实施负责。因此，业务合伙人负责审计计划工作，并且可以寻求适当的业务团队成员协助，以便履行该责任。协助业务合伙人制订审计计划的业务团队成员也需要遵守本准则的有关规定。

Planning an Audit
计划审计业务

4. The auditor should properly plan the audit. This standard describes the auditor's responsibilities for properly planning the audit. ②

4. 审计师应当合理地计划审计业务。本准则规定了审计师合理地计划审计业务的责任。

5. Planning the audit includes establishing the overall audit strategy for the engagement and developing an audit plan, which includes, in particular, planned risk assessment procedures and planned responses to the risks of material misstatement. Planning is not a discrete phase of an audit but, rather, a continual and iterative process that might begin shortly after (or in connection with) the completion of the previous audit and continues until the completion of the current audit.

5. 审计计划工作包括制定业务的总体审计策略和编制审计计划，包括预定风险评估程序和预定重大错报风险应对策略。计划与审计业务不可分离，而是一个持续和反复的过程，可能从上次审计完成之后（或紧接着上次审计）开始直至本次审计结束。

Preliminary Engagement Activities
前期业务活动

6. The auditor should perform the following activities at the beginning of the audit:

6. 审计师应当在审计业务开始时进行下列活动：

a. Perform procedures regarding the continuance of the client relationship and the specific audit engagement, ③

a. 实施与客户关系保持和本次特定审计业务有关的程序，

b. Determine compliance with independence and ethics requirements, and

b. 确定符合独立性和职业道德的规定，并且

Note: The determination of compliance with independence and ethics requirements is not limited to preliminary engagement activities and should be reevaluated with changes in circumstances.

注：确定符合独立性和职业道德的规定不仅限于前期业务活动，而且应当在环境变化时重新评价。

c. Establish an understanding of the terms of the audit engagement with the audit committee in accordance with Auditing Standard No. 16, Communications with Audit Committees. ④

c. 遵照审计准则第 16 号［与审计委员会的沟通］，对本次审计业务的条款与审计委员会达成共识。

Planning Activities
计划活动

7. The nature and extent of planning activities that are necessary depend on the size and complexity of the company, the auditor's previous experience with the company, and changes in circumstances that occur during the audit. When developing the audit strategy and audit plan, as discussed in paragraphs 8 – 10, the auditor should evaluate whether the following matters are important to the company's financial statements and internal control over financial reporting and, if so, how they will affect the auditor's procedures:

7. 必要的计划活动的性质和范围取决于公司的大小和复杂性、审计师以往的经验以及审计过程中的环境变化。在制定第 8 至 10 款所说的审计策略和审计计划时，审计师应当评价以下事项对于该公司财务报表和财务报告内部控制是否重要，如果重要，那么，这些事项将如何影响审计师的程序。

• Knowledge of the company's internal control over financial reporting obtained during other engagements performed by the auditor;

• 审计师在其实施的其他业务中获取的有关该公司财务报告内部控制的情况;

• Matters affecting the industry in which the company operates, such as financial reporting practices, economic conditions, laws and regulations, and technological changes;

• 影响该公司所处行业的事项,例如,财务报告实务,经营环境、法律和法规以及技术变化;

• Matters relating to the company's business, including its organization, operating characteristics, and capital structure;

• 该公司经营相关的事项,包括组织结构、运营特点和资本结构;

• The extent of recent changes, if any, in the company, its operations, or its internal control over financial reporting;

• 公司内部运营或财务报告内部控制近期变化的范围(如果有的话);

• The auditor's preliminary judgments about materiality,⑤ risk, and, in integrated audits, other factors relating to the determination of material weaknesses;

• 审计师对于重要性、风险和整合审计中决定实质性缺陷的其他因素的初步判断;

• Control deficiencies previously communicated to the audit committee⑥ or management;

• 曾经向审计委员会和管理层沟通过的控制缺陷;

• Legal or regulatory matters of which the company is aware;

• 公司已知的法律或监管事项;

• The type and extent of available evidence

• 与该公司财务报告内部

related to the effectiveness of the company's internal control over financial reporting;

控制有关的可用证据的类型和范围；

• Preliminary judgments about the effectiveness of internal control over financial reporting;

• 对于财务报告内部控制有效性的初步判断；

• Public information about the company relevant to the evaluation of the likelihood of material financial statement misstatements and the effectiveness of the company's internal control over financial reporting;

• 与该公司财务报表重大错报可能性和财务报告内部控制有效性有关的公开资料；

• Knowledge about risks related to the company evaluated as part of the auditor's client acceptance and retention evaluation; and

• 作为审计师接纳和保留客户的评价组成部分的有关该公司风险的知识；和

• The relative complexity of the company's operations.

• 该公司运营的相对复杂性。

Note: Many smaller companies have less complex operations. Additionally, some larger, complex companies may have less complex units or processes. Factors that might indicate less complex operations include: fewer business lines; less complex business processes and financial reporting systems; more centralized accounting functions; extensive involvement by senior management in the day-to-day activities of the business; and fe-

注：许多较小的公司运营不太复杂。另外，某些大型、复杂的公司可能有一些业务单元或过程不太复杂。表明运营不太复杂的因素包括：较少的业务部门；不太复杂的运营过程和财务报告系统；较多的集中化会计职能；高级管理层广泛地参与运营的日

wer levels of management, each with a wide span of control.

常活动；较少的管理层级，每个管理层级负责较大范围的控制。

Audit Strategy
审计策略

8. The auditor should establish an overall audit strategy that sets the scope, timing, and direction of the audit and guides the development of the audit plan.

8. 审计师应当制定总体审计策略，明确审计业务范围、时间和方向，以指导审计计划的编制。

9. In establishing the overall audit strategy, the auditor should take into account:

9. 对于制定总体审计策略，审计师应当考虑：

a. The reporting objectives of the engagement and the nature of the communications required by PCAOB standards, [7]

a. 本业务的报告目标和 PCAOB 准则要求的沟通性质，

b. The factors that are significant in directing the activities of the engagement team, [8]

b. 指引业务团队审计活动方向的重大因素，

c. The results of preliminary engagement activities[9] and the auditor's evaluation of the important matters in accordance with paragraph 7 of this standard, and

c. 前期业务活动的结果和审计师按照本准则第 7 款对于重大事项的评价，和

d. The nature, timing, and extent of resources necessary to perform the engagement. [10]

d. 实施本业务所需资源的性质、时间和范围。

Audit Plan
审计计划

10. The auditor should develop and document an audit plan that includes a description of:

10. 审计师应当编制和归档包括以下内容的审计计划

a. The planned nature, timing, and extent of the risk assessment procedures; ⑪

a. 风险评估程序中预定的性质、时间和范围；

b. The planned nature, timing, and extent of tests of controls and substantive procedures; ⑫ and

b. 控制测试和实质性程序中预定的性质、时间和范围；和

c. Other planned audit procedures required to be performed so that the engagement complies with PCAOB standards.

c. 为了使业务符合 PCAOB 准则而实施的其他预定审计程序。

Multi – location Engagements
多场所业务

11. In an audit of the financial statements of a company with operations in multiple locations or business units, ⑬ the auditor should determine the extent to which audit procedures should be performed at selected locations or business units to obtain sufficient appropriate evidence to obtain reasonable assurance about whether the consolidated financial

11. 对于在多场所运营或多业务单元的公司的财务报表审计，审计师应当确定在所选定场所或业务单元实施的程序的范围，以便取得充分适当的证据，合理地保证合并财务报表没有重大错报。这包括确

statements are free of material misstatement. This includes determining the locations or business units at which to perform audit procedures, as well as the nature, timing, and extent of the procedures to be performed at those individual locations or business units. The auditor should assess the risks of material misstatement to the consolidated financial statements associated with the location or business unit and correlate the amount of audit attention devoted to the location or business unit with the degree of risk of material misstatement associated with that location or business unit.

定实施审计程序的场所或业务单元，以及在每个场所或业务单元实施程序的性质、时间和范围。审计师应当评估与该场所或业务单元相关的合并财务报表重大错报风险，并且将分配给该场所或业务单元的审计关注与该场所或业务单元相关的重大错报风险程度关联起来。

12. Factors that are relevant to the assessment of the risks of material misstatement associated with a particular location or business unit and the determination of the necessary audit procedures include:

12. 与特定场所或业务单元的重大错报风险评估以及确定所需审计程序相关的因素包括：

a. The nature and amount of assets, liabilities, and transactions executed at the location or business unit, including, e. g. , significant transactions executed at the location or business unit that are outside the normal course of business for the company, or that otherwise appear to be unusual given the auditor's understanding of the company and its environment; ⑭

a. 该场所或业务单元的资产、负债和交易的性质和金额，包括，该场所或业务单元发生的在该公司正常业务之外重大交易，或者，就审计师对于该公司及其所处环境的理解而言显得不同寻常的交易；

b. The materiality of the location or business unit; [15]

b. 该场所或业务单元的重要性；

c. The specific risks associated with the location or business unit that present a reasonable possibility [16] of material misstatement to the company's consolidated financial statements;

c. 与该场所或业务单元相关的特有风险，这些风险对于造成该公司的合并财务报表重大错报而言具有合理的可能性；

d. Whether the risks of material misstatement associated with the location or business unit apply to other locations or business units such that, in combination, they present a reasonable possibility of material misstatement to the company's consolidated financial statements;

d. 与该场所或业务单元相关的重大错报风险是否适用于其他场所或业务单元，如果合并考虑，是否对于造成该公司的合并财务报表重大错报而言具有合理的可能性；

e. The degree of centralization of records or information processing;

e. 资料和信息处理的集中度；

f. The effectiveness of the control environment, particularly with respect to management's control over the exercise of authority delegated to others and its ability to effectively supervise activities at the location or business unit; and

f. 控制环境的有效性，尤其是管理层对于授权行为的控制以及有效监督该场所或业务单元活动的能力；和

g. The frequency, timing, and scope of monitoring activities by the company or others at the location or business unit.

g. 该公司或他人在该场所或业务单元进行的监控活动的频率、时间和范围。

Note: When performing an audit of internal control over financial reporting, refer to Appendix B, Special Topics, of Auditing Standard No. 5 [17] for considerations when a company has multiple locations or business units.

注：在考虑对具有多个场所或业务单元的公司实施财务报告内部控制审计时，参见审计准则第 5 号附件 B［特殊议题］。

13. In determining the locations or business units at which to perform audit procedures, the auditor may take into account relevant activities performed by internal audit, as described in AU sec. 322, The auditor's Consideration of the Internal Audit Function in an Audit of Financial Statements, or others, as described in Auditing Standard No. 5. AU sec. 322 and Auditing Standard No. 5 establish requirements regarding using the work of internal audit and others, respectively.

13. 在确定实施审计程序的场所或业务单元时，审计师可以将过渡性审计准则第 322 条［审计师对于内部审计职能在财务报告审计中的考虑］描述的内部审计部门实施的，或者，审计准则第 5 号描述的其他人员实施的相关活动考虑在内。过渡性审计准则第 322 条和审计准则第 5 号分别为利用内部审计人员和其他人员的工作制定要求。

14. AU sec. 543, Part of Audit Performed by Other Independent Auditors, describes the auditor's responsibilities regarding using the work and reports of other independent auditors who audit the financial statements of one or more of the locations or business units that are included in the consolidated financial statements. [18] In those situations, the auditor

14. 过渡性审计准则第 543 条［部分审计由其他独立审计师实施］规定了审计师在利用其他独立审计师的工作和报告时的责任，这些独立审计师审计的一个或多个场所或业务单元的财务报表包括在合

should perform the procedures in paragraphs 11 – 13 of this standard to determine the locations or business units at which audit procedures should be performed.

并财务报表中。在这些情况下，审计师应当实施本准则第 11 至 13 款的程序，确定应当实施审计程序的场所和业务单元。

Changes During the Course of the Audit
审计过程中的变化

15. The auditor should modify the overall audit strategy and the audit plan as necessary if circumstances change significantly during the course of the audit, including changes due to a revised assessment of the risks of material misstatement or the discovery of a previously unidentified risk of material misstatement.

15. 如果在审计过程中环境发生重大变化，包括重大错报风险的重新评估或者发现原来未识别的重大错报风险等引起的变化，审计师应当修订总体审计策略和审计计划。

Persons with Specialized Skill or Knowledge
具有特殊技能和知识的人员

16. The auditor should determine whether specialized skill or knowledge is needed to perform appropriate risk assessments, plan or perform audit procedures, or evaluate audit results.

16. 审计师应当确定是否需要特殊技能或知识，用于实施适当的风险评估、计划或实施审计程序或者评价审计结果。

17. If a person with specialized skill or knowledge employed or engaged by the auditor participates in the audit, the auditor should have sufficient knowledge of the sub-

17. 如果审计师雇用或聘用某位具有专业技术或知识的人员参与审计，审计师应当对该人员处理的鉴

ject matter to be addressed by such a person to enable the auditor to:

证事项具有足够的知识，使得审计师能够：

a. Communicate the objectives of that person's work;

a. 沟通该人员工作的目标；

b. Determine whether that person's procedures meet the auditor's objectives; and

b. 确定该人员的程序是否符合审计师的目标；和

c. Evaluate the results of that person's procedures as they relate to the nature, timing, and extent of other planned audit procedures and the effects on the auditor's report.

c. 评价该人员实施的程序的结果与其他预定审计程序的性质、时间和范围的关系，以及对审计报告的影响。

Additional Considerations in Initial Audits

初次审计的补充考虑

18. The auditor should undertake the following activities before starting an initial audit:

18. 审计师应当在开始初次审计之前进行下列工作：

a. Perform procedures regarding the acceptance of the client relationship and the specific audit engagement; and

a. 针对客户关系接纳和特定审计业务实施程序；和

b. Communicate with the predecessor auditor in situations in which there has been a change of auditors in accordance with AU sec. 315, Communications Between Predecessor and Successor Auditors.

b. 对于已经发生审计师变更的情况，遵照过渡性审计准则第315条［前任和后任审计师之间的沟通］，与前任审计师沟通。

19. The purpose and objective of planning the audit are the same for an initial audit or a recurring audit engagement. However, for an initial audit, the auditor should determine the additional planning activities necessary to establish an appropriate audit strategy and audit plan, including determining the audit procedures necessary to obtain sufficient appropriate audit evidence regarding the opening balances. ⑲

19. 初次审计或连续审计业务的审计计划工作的目的和目标是相同的。但是，对于初次审计，审计师应当确定为了制定适当的审计策略和审计计划所需的补充计划活动，包括确定为获取充分适当的期初余额审计证据所需的审计程序。

① Terms defined in Appendix A, Definitions, are set in **boldface type** the first time they appear.

附录 A［定义］定义的用语首次出现时采用**粗体字**。

② The term, "auditor," as used in this standard, encompasses both the engagement partner and the engagement team members who assist the engagement partner in planning the audit.

本准则的“审计师”包括业务合伙人和协助业务合伙人制订审计计划的业务团队成员。

③ Paragraphs . 14 – . 16 of QC sec. 20, System of Quality Control for a CPA Firm's Accounting and Auditing Practice. AU sec. 161, The Relationship of Generally Accepted Auditing Standards to Quality Control Standards, explains how the quality control standards relate to the conduct of audits.

过渡性审计准则第 151 条［公认审计准则与质量控制准则的关系］的质量控制第 20 条［会计事务所会计和审计业务的质量控制系统］第 . 14 至 . 16 款解释了质量控制系统与审计业务的关系。

④［Footnote deleted, effective for audits of fiscal years beginning on or after December 15, 2012. See PCAOB Release No. 2012 – 004.］

［由于本脚注已不适用于 2012 年 12 月 15 日（含）开始的会计年度审计，因此删除。参见 PCAOB 第 2012 – 004 号公告。］

⑤ Auditing Standard No. 11, Consideration of Materiality in Planning and Performing an Audit.

审计准则第 11 号［在计划和实施审计时对于重要性的考虑］

⑥ If no audit committee exists, all references to the audit committee in this standard apply to the entire board of directors of the company. See 15 U. S. C. § § 78c（a）58 and 7201（a）（3）.

如果没有审计委员会，本准则所指的审计委员会均为公司的整个董事会。参见 15 U. S. C. § § 78c（a）58 and 7201（a）（3）。

⑦ See, e. g. , Auditing Standard No. 16, Communications with Audit Committees. Also, various laws or regulations require other matters to be communicated. (See, e. g. , Rule 2 – 07 of Regulation S – X, 17 CFR 210. 2 – 07; and Rule 10A – 3 under the Securities Exchange Act of 1934, 17 CFR 240. 10A – 3.) The requirements of this standard do not modify communications required by those other laws or regulations.

参见审计准则第 16 号［与审计委员会的沟通］。而且，各种法律和法规也需要沟通其他事项。(参见 Rule 2 – 07 of Regulation S – X, 17 CFR 210. 2 – 07; 和 Rule 10A – 3 under the Securities Exchange Act of 1934, 17 CFR 240. 10A – 3。) 本准则的要求不改变那些其他法律和法规所要求的沟通。

⑧ See, e. g. , paragraph 6 of Auditing Standard No. 10, Supervision of the Audit Engagement.

参见审计准则第 10 号［审计业务的监督］第 6 款

⑨ Paragraph 6 of this standard.

本准则第 6 款

⑩ See, e. g. , paragraph . 06 of AU sec. 230, Due Professional Care in the Performance of Work, paragraph 16 of this standard, and paragraph 5. a. of Auditing Standard No. 13, The auditor's Responses to the Risks of Material Misstatement.

参见过渡性审计准则第 230 条［业务实施中的职业审慎］第 . 06 款、本准则第 16 款和审计准则第 13 号［审计师对于重大错报风险的应对策略］第 5. a 款。

⑪ Auditing Standard No. 12, Identifying and Assessing Risks of Material Misstatement.

审计准则第 12 号［识别和评估重大错报风险］

⑫ Auditing Standard No. 13 and Auditing Standard No. 5, An Audit of Internal Control Over Financial Reporting That Is Integrated with An Audit of Financial Statements.

审计准则第 13 号和审计准则第 5 号［与财务报表审计合并执行的财务报告内部控制审计］。

⑬ The term "business units" includes subsidiaries, divisions, branches, components, or investments.

"业务单元"包括子公司、事业部、分公司、部门或对外投资。

⑭ Paragraph . 66 of AU sec. 316, Consideration of Fraud in a Financial Statement Audit.

过渡性审计准则第 316 条［财务报表审计中的舞弊考虑］第 . 66 款

⑮ Paragraph 10 of Auditing Standard No. 11 describes the consideration of materiality in planning and performing audit procedures at an individual location or business unit.

审计准则第 11 号第 10 款描述了在个别营业场所或业务单元计划和实施审计程序时对于重要性的考虑。

⑯ There is a reasonable possibility of an event, as used in this standard, when the likelihood of the event is either "reasonably possible" or "probable," as those terms are used in the FASB Accounting Standards Codification, Contingencies Topic, paragraph 450 – 20 – 25 – 1.

本准则所称某事件存在合理的可能性是指该事件的发生要么"合理的可能"，要么"有可能"，这两个词汇的定义与美国财务会计准则委员会"会计准则汇编"［或有事项］第 450 – 20 – 25 – 1 款的定义一致。

⑰ Paragraphs B10 – B16 of Auditing Standard No. 5.

审计准则第 5 号第 B10 – B16 款。

⑱ For integrated audits, see also paragraphs C8 – C11 of Auditing Standard No. 5.

关于整合审计，参见审计准则第 5 号第 C8 至 C11 款。

⑲ See also paragraph 3 of Auditing Standard No. 6, Evaluating Consistency of Financial Statements.

参见审计准则第 6 号［评价财务报表的一致性］第 3 款。

Appendix A Definitions

附录A －定义

A1. For purposes of this standard, the term listed below is defined as follows:

A1. 就本准则而言，下列用语的定义是：

A2. Engagement partner – The member of the engagement team with primary responsibility for the audit.

A2. 业务合伙人是承担审计业务首要责任的业务团队成员。

December 15, 2010

2010 年 12 月 15 日

AUDITING AND RELATED PROFESSIONAL PRACTICE STANDARDS

审计及相关专业实务准则

Auditing Standard No. 10 –

审计准则第 10 号 —

Supervision of the Audit Engagement

审计业务的监督

PCAOB

Public Company Accounting Oversight Board

公众公司会计监管委员会

[Effective pursuant to SEC Release No. 34 – 63606, File No. PCAOB – 2010 – 01, December 23, 2010]

[按照 SEC 第 34 – 63606 号公告生效；文件号：PCAOB – 2010 – 01，2012 年 12 月 23 日]

Final Rule：PCAOB Release No. 2010 – 004

最终规则：PCAOB 公告第 2010 – 004 号

Table of Contents

目　　录

Paragraph

款　　号

Introduction
引　言

1. This standard establishes requirements regarding supervision of the audit engagement, including supervising the work of engagement team members.

1. 本准则为审计业务监督制定要求，包括监督业务团队成员的工作。

Objective
目　标

2. The objective of the auditor is to supervise the audit engagement, including supervising the work of engagement team members so that the work is performed as directed and supports the conclusions reached.

2. 审计师的目标是监督审计业务，包括监督业务团队成员的工作，使其工作按照要求进行，并支持得出的结论。

Responsibility of the Engagement Partner for Supervision
业务合伙人的监督责任

3. **The engagement partner**① is responsible for the engagement and its performance. Accordingly, the engagement partner is responsible for proper supervision of the work of engagement team members and for compliance with PCAOB standards, including standards regarding using the work of spe-

3. 业务合伙人对业务及其实施负责。因此，业务合伙人对业务团队成员工作的适当监督和遵守 PCAOB 准则负责，包括遵守有关利用专家、其他审计师、内部审计师和其

cialists, [2] other auditors, [3] internal auditors, [4] and others who are involved in testing controls. [5] Paragraphs 5 – 6 of this standard describe the nature and extent of supervisory activities necessary for proper supervision of engagement team members. [6]

他参与控制测试人员的工作的准则。本准则第 5 至 6 款描述业务团队成员适当监督所需的监督活动的性质和范围。

4. The engagement partner may seek assistance from appropriate engagement team members in fulfilling his or her responsibilities pursuant to this standard. Engagement team members who assist the engagement partner with supervision of the work of other engagement team members also should comply with the requirements in this standard with respect to the supervisory responsibilities assigned to them.

4. 业务合伙人可以向适当的业务团队成员寻求帮助，从而满足本准则对其责任的要求。协助业务合伙人监督其他业务团队成员工作的业务团队成员也应当符合本准则有关分派给他们的监督责任的规定。

Supervision of Engagement Team Members

业务团队成员的监督

5. The engagement partner and, as applicable, other engagement team members performing supervisory activities, should:

5. 业务合伙人和（在适用条件下）执行监督活动的其他业务团队成员应当：

a. Inform engagement team members of their responsibilities, [7] including:

a. 告知业务团队成员其责任，包括：

(1) The objectives of the procedures that they are to perform;

（1）将要实施的程序的目标；

(2) The nature, timing, and extent of procedures they are to perform; and

(2) 将要实施的程序的性质、时间和范围；和

(3) Matters that could affect the procedures to be performed or the evaluation of the results of those procedures, including relevant aspects of the company, its environment, and its internal control over financial reporting, ⑧ and possible accounting and auditing issues;

(3) 可能影响将要实施的程序或者这些程序的结果评价的事项，包括公司及其环境和财务报告内部控制的有关方面，以及可能的会计和审计问题；

b. Direct engagement team members to bring significant accounting and auditing issues arising during the audit to the attention of the engagement partner or other engagement team members performing supervisory activities so they can evaluate those issues and determine that appropriate actions are taken in accordance with PCAOB standards; ⑨

b. 指示业务团队成员将审计中出现的重大会计和审计问题提请业务合伙人或其他执行监督活动的业务团队成员注意，以便他们评价这些问题，并确定按照 PCAOB 准则采取适当的行动。

Note: In applying due professional care in accordance with AU sec. 230, each engagement team member has a responsibility to bring to the attention of appropriate persons, disagreements or concerns the engagement team member might have with respect to accounting and auditing issues that he or she believes are of significance to the financial statements or the auditor's report regardless of how those disagreements or concerns may have arisen.

注：为了按照过渡性审计准则第 230 条运用职业审慎，每位业务团队成员均有责任将其认为对于财务报表或审计报告而言重大的会计或审计问题的不同意见或需关注事项提请适当人员注意，而不论这些不同意见或需关注事项是如何产生的。

c. Review the work of engagement team members to evaluate whether:

c. 复核业务团队成员的工作以便评价：

(1) The work was performed and documented;

(1) 其工作是否实施和存档；

(2) The objectives of the procedures were achieved; and

(2) 程序的目标是否达成；和

(3) The results of the work support the conclusions reached. ⑩

(3) 工作的结果是否支持得出的结论。

6. To determine the extent of supervision necessary for engagement team members to perform their work as directed and form appropriate conclusions, the engagement partner and other engagement team members performing supervisory activities should take into account:

6. 为了确定业务团队成员按照指示执行工作并形成适当结论所需的监督范围，业务合伙人和执行监督活动的其他业务团队成员应当考虑：

a. The nature of the company, including its size and complexity; ⑪

a. 公司的性质，包括其大小和复杂性；

b. The nature of the assigned work for each engagement team member, including:

b. 分派给每位业务团队成员的工作的性质，包括：

(1) The procedures to be performed, and
(2) The controls or accounts and disclosures to be tested;

(1) 实施的程序，和
(2) 将要测试的控制或账户和披露；

c. The risks of material misstatement; and

c. 重大错报风险；和

d. The knowledge, skill, and ability of each engagement team member. [12]

d. 每位业务团队成员的知识、技能和能力。

Note: In accordance with the requirements of paragraph 5 of Auditing Standard No. 13, The auditor's Responses to the Risks of Material Misstatement, the extent of supervision of engagement team members should be commensurate with the risks of material misstatement. [13]

注：按照审计准则第 13 号［审计师对于重大错报风险的应对策略］第 5 款的要求，业务团队成员的监督范围应当与重大错报风险相一致。

---

① Terms defined in Appendix A, Definitions, are set in **boldface type** the first time they appear.

附录 A［定义］定义的用语首次出现时采用**粗体字**。

② AU sec. 336, Using the Work of a Specialist.

过渡性审计准则第 336 条［利用专家的工作］

③ AU sec. 543, Part of Audit Performed by Other Independent Auditors.

过渡性审计准则第 543 条［部分审计由其他独立审计师实施］

④ AU sec. 322, The auditor's Consideration of the Internal Audit Function in an Audit of Financial Statements.

过渡性审计准则第 322 条［审计师对于内部审计职能在财务报告审计中的考虑］

⑤ Paragraphs 16 – 19 of Auditing Standard No. 5, An Audit of Internal Control Over Financial Reporting That Is Integrated with An Audit of Financial Statements.

审计准则第 5 号［与财务报表审计合并执行的财务报告内部控制审计］第 16 至 19 款

⑥ See also paragraph .06 of AU sec. 230, Due Professional Care in the Performance of Work.

参见过渡性审计准则第 230 条［业务实施中的职业审慎］第 .06 款

⑦ AU sec. 230.06 and paragraph 5 of Auditing Standard No. 13, The auditor's Responses to the Risks of Material Misstatement, establish requirements regarding the appropriate assignment of engagement team members.

过渡性审计准则第 230 条第 .06 款和审计准则第 13 号［审计师对于重大错报风险的应对策略］为适当地分派业务团队成员制定要求。

⑧ Auditing Standard No. 12, Identifying and Assessing Risks of Material Misstatement, describes the auditor's responsibilities for obtaining an understanding of the company, its environment, and its internal control over financial reporting.

审计准则第 12 号［识别和评估重大错报风险］规定了审计师了解公司及其所在环境和财务报

告内部控制的责任。

⑨ See , e. g. , paragraph 15 of Auditing Standard No. 9, Audit Planning, paragraph 74 of Auditing Standard No. 12, and paragraphs 20 – 23 and 35 – 36 of Auditing Standard No. 14, Evaluating Audit Results.

审计准则第 9 号［审计计划］第 15 款、审计准则第 12 号第 74 款和审计准则第 14 号［评价审计结果］第 20 至 23 款和第 35 至 36 款。

⑩ Auditing Standard No. 14 describes the auditor's responsibilities for evaluating the results of the audit, and Auditing Standard No. 3, Audit Documentation, establishes requirements regarding audit documentation.

审计准则第 14 号规定了审计师评价审计结果的责任，审计准则第 3 号［审计文档］为审计文档制定要求。

⑪ Paragraph 10 of Auditing Standard No. 12.

审计准则第 12 号第 10 款

⑫ See also paragraph 5. a. of Auditing Standard No. 13 and AU sec. 230. 06.

参见审计准则第 13 号第 5. a. 款和过渡性审计准则第 230. 06 款

⑬ Paragraph 5. b. of Auditing Standard No. 13 indicates that the extent of supervision of engagement team members is part of the auditor's overall responses to the risks of material misstatement.

审计准则第 13 号第 5. b. 款指出对于业务团队成员的监督范围是审计师对于重大错报风险总体应对策略的一部分。

Appendix A Definitions

附录A －定义

A1. For purposes of this standard, the term listed below is defined as follows:

A1. 就本准则而言，下列用语的定义是：

A2. Engagement partner – The member of the engagement team with primary responsibility for the audit.

A2. 业务合伙人是承担审计业务首要责任的业务团队成员。

December 15, 2010

2010 年 12 月 15 日

AUDITING AND RELATED PROFESSIONAL PRACTICE STANDARDS

审计及相关专业实务准则

Auditing Standard No. 11 –

审计准则第 11 号 —

Consideration of Materiality in Planning and Performing an Audit

在计划和实施审计时对于重要性的考虑

PCAOB

Public Company Accounting Oversight Board

公众公司会计监管委员会

[Effective pursuant to SEC Release No. 34 –63606, File No. PCAOB –2010 –01, December 23, 2010]

[按照 SEC 第 34 –63606 号公告生效；文件号：PCAOB –2010 –01，2012 年 12 月 23 日]

Final Rule：PCAOB Release No. 2010 –004

最终规则：PCAOB 公告第 2010 –004 号

Table of Contents

目 录

Paragraph

款 号

Introduction
引 言

1. This standard establishes requirements regarding the auditor's consideration of materiality in planning and performing an audit. ①

1. 本准则为审计师在计划和实施审计时考虑重要性制定要求。

Materiality in the Context of an Audit
审计领域的重要性

2. In interpreting the federal securities laws, the Supreme Court of the United States has held that a fact is material if there is "a substantial likelihood that the …fact would have been viewed by the reasonable investor as having significantly altered the 'total mix' of information made available." ② As the Supreme Court has noted, determinations of materiality require "delicate assessments of the inferences a 'reasonable shareholder' would draw from a given set of facts and the significance of those inferences to him …" ③

2. 在解释联邦证券法律时，美国最高法院认为如果"理性投资者极有可能认为某事实已经显著改变了可用信息的'总体含义'"，那么，该事实就是重要的。最高法院指出，重要性的确定需要"细致分析'理性投资者'从一组给定事实中可能得出的推论及其对于该投资者的重大性……"。

3. To obtain reasonable assurance about whether the financial statements are free of material misstatement, the auditor should plan and perform audit procedures to detect misstatements that, individually or in combination with other misstatements, would result

3. 为了获得财务报表是否没有重大错报的合理保证，审计师应当计划和实施审计程序，发现单独或与连同其他错报一起可能导致财务报表重大错报的

in material misstatement of the financial statements. This includes being alert while planning and performing audit procedures for misstatements that could be material due to quantitative or qualitative factors. Also, the evaluation of uncorrected misstatements in accordance with Auditing Standard No. 14, Evaluating Audit Results, requires consideration of both qualitative and quantitative factors. ④ However, it ordinarily is not practical to design audit procedures to detect misstatements that are material based solely on qualitative factors.

错报。这包括在计划和实施审计程序时对于那些由于数量或质量因素而重大的错报保持警惕。另外，遵循审计准则第 14 号［评价审计结果］执行的未纠正错报的评价要求同时考虑数量和质量因素。但是，为了发现仅从质量因素方面看来是重大的错报而设计审计程序，通常是不可行的。

4. For integrated audits, Auditing Standard No. 5, An Audit of Internal Control Over Financial Reporting That Is Integrated with An Audit of Financial Statements, states, "In planning the audit of internal control over financial reporting, the auditor should use the same materiality considerations he or she would use in planning the audit of the company's annual financial statements." ⑤

4. 对于整合审计，审计准则第 5 号［与财务报表审计合并执行的财务报告内部控制审计］指出"在计划财务报表内部控制审计时，审计师应当采用与其计划该公司年度财务报表审计相同的重要性。"

Objective
目　标

5. The objective of the auditor is to apply the concept of materiality appropriately in planning and performing audit procedures.

5. 审计师的目标是在计划和实施审计程序时运用合理的重要性。

Considering Materiality in Planning and Performing an Audit
在计划和实施审计时考虑重要性

Establishing a Materiality Level for the Financial Statements as a Whole
确定财务报表总体重要性

6. To plan the nature, timing, and extent of audit procedures, the auditor should establish a materiality level for the financial statements as a whole that is appropriate in light of the particular circumstances. This includes consideration of the company's earnings and other relevant factors. To determine the nature, timing, and extent of audit procedures, the materiality level for the financial statements as a whole needs to be expressed as a specified amount.

6. 为了计划审计程序的性质、时间和范围，审计师应当根据具体情况确定适当的财务报表总体重要性。这包括该公司的盈利及其他相关因素。为了确定审计程序的性质、时间和范围，需要将财务报表总体重要性表述为一个明确的金额。

Note: If financial statements for the audit period are not available, the auditor may establish an initial materiality level based on estimated or preliminary financial statement amounts. In those situations, the auditor should take into account the effects of known or expected changes in the company's financial statements, including significant transactions or adjustments that are expected to be reflected in the financial statements at the

注：如果没有该审计期间的财务报表，审计师可以基于估计或初步财务报表金额确定一个初始重要性。在这些情况下，审计师应当将该公司财务报表中已知或预期的变化考虑在内，包括将要在期末反映到该财务报表中的重大交易或调整。

end of the period.

Establishing Materiality Levels for Particular Accounts or Disclosures
为特定账户或披露确定重要性

7. The auditor should evaluate whether, in light of the particular circumstances, there are certain accounts or disclosures for which there is a substantial likelihood that misstatements of lesser amounts than the materiality level established for the financial statements as a whole would influence the judgment of a reasonable investor. If so, the auditor should establish separate materiality levels for those accounts or disclosures to plan the nature, timing, and extent of audit procedures for those accounts or disclosures.

7. 审计师应当根据具体情况评价，对于某些账户或披露而言，低于财务报表总体重要性的错报是否极有可能影响某位理性投资者的判断。如果需要，那么，审计师应当为这些账户或披露制定单独的重要性，用于为这些账户或披露计划审计程序的性质、时间和范围。

Note：Lesser amounts of misstatements could influence the judgment of a reasonable investor because of qualitative factors, e. g. , because of the sensitivity of circumstances surrounding misstatements, such as conflicts of interest in related party transactions.

较低金额的错报会由于其质的因素而影响某位理性投资者的判断，例如，错报所在环境的严重性，比如，在关联方交易中的利益冲突。

Determining Tolerable Misstatement
确定可容忍错报

8. The auditor should determine the amount or amounts of tolerable misstatement for purposes

8. 审计师应当为评估重大错报风险以及计划和实

of assessing risks of material misstatement and planning and performing audit procedures at the account or disclosure level. The auditor should determine tolerable misstatement at an amount or amounts that reduce to an appropriately low level the probability that the total of uncorrected and undetected misstatements would result in material misstatement of the financial statements. Accordingly, tolerable misstatement should be less than the materiality level for the financial statements as a whole and, if applicable, the materiality level or levels for particular accounts or disclosures.

施账户或披露层次审计程序确定可容忍错报的金额。审计师应当确定一个或多个可容忍错报金额，将可能导致财务报表重大错报的未纠正和未发现错报的概率降到适当的低水平。因此，可容忍错报应当低于财务报表总体重要性和（如果适用的话）特定账户或披露的重要性。

9. In determining tolerable misstatement and planning and performing audit procedures, the auditor should take into account the nature, cause (if known), and amount of misstatements that were accumulated in audits of the financial statements of prior periods.

9. 在确定可容忍错报以及计划和实施审计程序时，审计师应当将以前期间的财务报表审计累计发现错报的性质、原因（如果知道的话）和金额考虑在内。

Considerations for Multi - location Engagements

多场所业务的考虑

10. For purposes of the audit of the consolidated financial statements of a company with multiple locations or business units, the auditor should determine tolerable misstatement for the individual locations or business units

10. 对于具有多个场所或业务单元公司的合并财务报表审计，审计师应当为个别场所或业务单元确定可容忍错报金额，该金额

at an amount that reduces to an appropriately low level the probability that the total of uncorrected and undetected misstatements would result in material misstatement of the consolidated financial statements. Accordingly, tolerable misstatement at an individual location should be less than the materiality level for the financial statements as a whole.

将可能导致财务报表重大错报的未纠正和未发现错报的概率降到适当的低水平。因此，个别场所的可容忍错报金额应当低于财务报表总体重要性。

Considerations as the Audit Progresses

审计进程中的考虑

11. The auditor should reevaluate the established materiality level or levels and tolerable misstatement when, because of changes in the particular circumstances or additional information that comes to the auditor's attention, there is a substantial likelihood that misstatements of amounts that differ significantly from the materiality level or levels that were established initially would influence the judgment of a reasonable investor. Situations in which changes in circumstances or additional information that comes to the auditor's attention would require such reevaluation include:

11. 当具体情况发生变化或者审计师发现进一步资料时，错报金额极有可能严重偏离最初确定的可能影响某位理性投资者判断的重要性，审计师应当重新评价确定的重要性和可容忍错报金额。由于具体情况变化或者审计师发现进一步资料而需要重新评价的那些情形包括：

a. The materiality level or levels and tolerable misstatement were established initially based on estimated or preliminary financial state-

a. 基于估计和初步财务报表金额确定的初始重要性和可容忍错报严重偏离

ment amounts that differ significantly from actual amounts.

实际金额。

b. Events or changes in conditions occurring after the materiality level or levels and tolerable misstatement were established initially are likely to affect investors' perceptions about the company's financial position, results of operations, or cash flows.

b. 在确定初始重要性和可容忍错报之后发生的时间或变更可能影响投资者对于该公司的财务状况、运营结果或现金流量的看法。

Note: Examples of such events or changes in conditions include (1) changes in laws, regulations, or the applicable financial reporting framework that affect investors' expectations about the measurement or disclosure of certain items and (2) significant new contractual arrangements that draw attention to a particular aspect of a company's business that is separately disclosed in the financial statements.

注：这些事件或变更包括（1）影响投资者对于某些财务报表项目的计量或披露的法律、法规或适用的财务报告框架的变更和（2）在财务报表中单独披露的引起对于某公司特定方面应予以关注的重大的新的合同安排。

12. If the auditor's reevaluation results in a lower amount for the materiality level or levels or tolerable misstatement than initially established by the auditor, the auditor should (1) evaluate the effect, if any, of the lower amount or amounts on his or her risk assessments and audit procedures and (2) modify the nature , timing , and extent of audit procedures as necessary to obtain sufficient ap-

12. 如果审计师的重新评价降低了其初始确定的重要性或可容忍错报，审计师应当（1）评价该较低金额对于其风险评估和审计程序的影响（如果有的话），和（2）修改审计程序的性质、时间和范围，以便获取充分适当的

propriate audit evidence.

审计证据。

Note: The reevaluation of the materiality level or levels and tolerable misstatement is also relevant to the auditor's evaluation of uncorrected misstatements in accordance with Auditing Standard No. 14. [6]

注：重新评价重要性或可容忍错报也与审计师按照审计准则第 14 号评价未纠正错报相关。

---

① Auditing Standard No. 14 establishes requirements regarding the auditor's consideration of materiality in evaluating audit results.

审计准则第 14 号为审计师评价审计结果时对于重要性的考虑制定要求。

② TSC Industries v. Northway, Inc. , 426 U. S. 438, 449 (1976). See also Basic, Inc. v. Levinson, 485 U. S. 224 (1988) .

TSC 工业公司诉 Northway 公司，426 U. S. 438，449（1976）。参见 Basic 公司诉 Levinson，485 U. S. 224（1988）。

③ TSC Industries, 426 U. S. at 450.

TSC 工业公司，426 U. S. at 450

④ Appendix B of Auditing Standard No. 14.

审计准则第 14 号附录 B

⑤ Paragraph 20 of Auditing Standard No. 5.

审计准则第 5 号第 20 款

⑥ Paragraph 17 of Auditing Standard No. 14.

审计准则第 14 号第 17 款

December 15, 2010
2010 年 12 月 15 日

AUDITING AND RELATED PROFESSIONAL PRACTICE STANDARDS
审计及相关专业实务准则

Auditing Standard No. 12 –
审计准则第 12 号 —

Identifying and Assessing Risks of Material Misstatement
识别和评估重大错报风险

PCAOB

Public Company Accounting Oversight Board
公众公司会计监管委员会

[Effective pursuant to SEC Release No. 34 – 63606, File No. PCAOB – 2010 – 01, December 23, 2010]
[按照 SEC 第 34 – 63606 号公告生效；文件号：PCAOB – 2010 – 01，2012 年 12 月 23 日]

Final Rule: PCAOB Release No. 2010 – 004
最终规则：PCAOB 公告第 2010 – 004 号

Table of Contents

目　　录

Paragraph

款　　号

Introduction
引　　言

1. This standard establishes requirements regarding the process of identifying and assessing risks of material misstatement[①] of the financial statements.

1. 本准则为识别和评估财务报表重大错报风险过程制定要求。

2. Paragraphs 4 – 58 of this standard discuss the auditor's responsibilities for performing **risk assessment procedures**.[②] Paragraphs 59 – 73 of this standard discuss identifying and assessing the risks of material misstatement using information obtained from performing risk assessment procedures.

2. 本准则第 4 至 58 款讨论审计师实施风险评估程序的责任。本准则第 59 至 73 款讨论利用实施**风险评估程序**获取的资料识别和评估重大错报风险。

Objective
目　　标

3. The objective of the auditor is to identify and appropriately assess the risks of material misstatement, thereby providing a basis for designing and implementing responses to the risks of material misstatement.

3. 审计师的目标是识别和适当地评估重大错报风险，从而为设计和执行重大错报风险应对策略提供基础。

Performing Risk Assessment Procedures
实施风险评估程序

4. The auditor should perform risk assessment

4. 审计师应当实施充分

procedures that are sufficient to provide a reasonable basis for identifying and assessing the risks of material misstatement, whether due to error or fraud, [3] and designing further audit procedures. [4]

的风险评估程序，为识别和评估由错误或舞弊造成的重大错报风险以及设计进一步审计程序提供合理基础。

5. Risks of material misstatement can arise from a variety of sources, including external factors, such as conditions in the company's industry and environment, and company-specific factors, such as the nature of the company, its activities, and internal control over financial reporting. For example, external or company-specific factors can affect the judgments involved in determining accounting estimates or create pressures to manipulate the financial statements to achieve certain financial targets. Also, risks of material misstatement may relate to, e. g., personnel who lack the necessary financial reporting competencies, information systems that fail to accurately capture business transactions, or financial reporting processes that are not adequately aligned with the requirements in the applicable financial reporting framework. Thus, the audit procedures that are necessary to identify and appropriately assess the risks of material misstatement include consideration of both external factors and company-specific factors. This standard

5. 重大错报风险有各种根源，包括外部因素，比如，公司所处行业和环境的状况，公司特有因素，比如，公司的性质、业务和财务报告内部控制。举例来说，外部和公司特有的因素可能影响涉及确定会计估计的判断，或者，产生为达成特定财务目标而操纵财务报表的压力。另外，重大错报风险可能与员工缺乏必要的财务报告胜任能力、信息系统未能准确捕捉业务交易、或者财务报告过程没有充分遵守适用的财务报告框架的要求等有关。因此，识别和适当地评估重大错报风险的审计程序包括对于外部和公司特有因素的考虑。本准则讨论下列风险评估程序：

discusses the following risk assessment procedures:

a. Obtaining an understanding of the company and its environment (paragraphs 7 – 17);

b. Obtaining an understanding of internal control over financial reporting (paragraphs 18 – 40);

c. Considering information from the client acceptance and retention evaluation, audit planning activities, past audits, and other engagements performed for the company (paragraphs 41 – 45);

d. Performing analytical procedures (paragraphs 46 – 48);

e. Conducting a discussion among engagement team members regarding the risks of material misstatement (paragraphs 49 – 53); and

f. Inquiring of the audit committee, management, and others within the company about the risks of material misstatement (paragraphs 54 – 58).

Note: This standard describes an approach to identifying and assessing risks of material

a. 了解公司及其环境（第7至17款）；

b. 了解财务报告内部控制（第18至40款）；

c. 考虑接纳和保留客户的评价、审计计划活动、以往审计和对该公司实施的其他业务中取得的资料（第41至45款）；

d. 实施分析性程序（第46至48款）；

e. 就重大错报风险在业务团队成员间讨论（第49至53款）；和

f. 就重大错报风险询问审计委员会、管理层和公司中的其他人员（第54至58款）。

注：本准则描述识别和评估重大错报风险的一种方

misstatement that begins at the financial statement level and with the auditor's overall understanding of the company and its environment and works down to the significant accounts and disclosures and their relevant assertions. ⑤

法，它从财务报表层次和审计师了解公司及其环境开始，直至重要账户和披露及其相关认定。

6. In an integrated audit, the risks of material misstatement of the financial statements are the same for both the audit of internal control over financial reporting and the audit of financial statements. The auditor's risk assessment procedures should apply to both the audit of internal control over financial reporting and the audit of financial statements.

6. 在整合审计中，财务报表重大错报风险与财务报告内部控制审计和财务报表审计的一样，审计师的风险评估程序应当同样适用于财务报告内部控制审计和财务报表审计。

Obtaining an Understanding of the Company and Its Environment
了解公司及其所处环境

7. The auditor should obtain an understanding of the company and its environment ("understanding of the company") to understand the events, conditions, and company activities that might reasonably be expected to have a significant effect on the risks of material misstatement. Obtaining an understanding of the company includes understanding:

7. 审计师应当了解公司及其环境（"了解公司"），从而了解那些可以被合理地预期将对重大错报风险产生重大影响的时间、状况和公司活动。了解公司包括：

a. Relevant industry, regulatory, and other external factors;

a. 相关的行业、监管和其他外部因素；

b. The nature of the company;

b. 公司的性质；

c. The company's selection and application of accounting principles, including related disclosures;

c. 公司会计政策及其相关披露的选择和运用；

d. **The company's objectives** and **strategies** and those related **business risks** that might reasonably be expected to result in risks of material misstatement; and

d. 可以被合理地预期将导致重大错报风险的那些**公司目标和战略**及其相关**经营风险**；和

e. The company's measurement and analysis of its financial performance.

e. 公司对于其财务表现的计量和分析。

8. In obtaining an understanding of the company, the auditor should evaluate whether significant changes in the company from prior periods , including changes in its internal control over financial reporting, affect the risks of material misstatement.

8. 在了解公司时，审计师应当评价公司与前期相比发生的重大变化，包括其财务报告内部控制，是否影响重大错报风险。

Industry , Regulatory , and Other External Factors

行业、监管和其他外部因素

9. Obtaining an understanding of relevant industry, regulatory, and other external factors encompasses industry factors , including the

9. 了解相关的行业、监管和其他外部因素涵盖行业因素，包括竞争环境和

competitive environment and technological developments; the regulatory environment, including the applicable financial reporting framework[6] and the legal and political environment; [7] and external factors, including general economic conditions.

技术发展；监管环境，包括适用的财务报告框架和法律及政治环境；和外部因素，包括总体经济状况。

Nature of the Company

公司的性质

10. Obtaining an understanding of the nature of the company includes understanding:

10. 了解公司的性质包括：

- The company's organizational structure and management personnel;

- 公司的组织结构和管理人员；

- The sources of funding of the company's operations and investment activities, including the company's capital structure, noncapital funding (e. g. , subordinated debt or dependencies on supplier financing) , and other debt instruments;

- 公司经营和投资活动的资金来源，包括公司的资本结构、非资本筹资（比如，次级债务或对于供应商筹资的依赖），和其他债务工具；

- The company's significant investments, including equity method investments, joint ventures, and variable interest entities;

- 公司的重大投资，包括权益法投资、合资和可变利益实体；

- The company's operating characteristics, including its size and complexity;

- 公司经营特点，包括规模大小和复杂性；

Note: The size and complexity of a company might affect the risks of misstatement and how the company addresses those risks.	• 注：公司的大小和复杂性会影响错报风险和公司如何处理这些风险。
• The sources of the company's earnings, including the relative profitability of key products and services; and	• 公司收入的来源，包括关键产品和服务的相对盈利能力；和
• Key supplier and customer relationships.	• 关键供应商以及客户关系。
Note: The auditor should take into account the information gathered while obtaining an understanding of the nature of the company when determining the existence of related parties in accordance with AU sec. 334, Related Parties.	注：审计师应当在按照过渡性审计准则第 334 条［关联方］确定关联方的存在性时，将了解公司性质时获取的资料考虑在内。
11. As part of obtaining an understanding of the company as required by paragraph 7, the auditor should consider performing the following procedures and the extent to which the procedures should be performed:	11. 作为第 7 款要求的了解公司的一部分，审计师应当考虑实施以下程序及其范围：
• Reading public information about the company relevant to the evaluation of the likelihood of material financial statement misstatements and, in an integrated audit, the effectiveness of the company's internal control over financial reporting, e. g., company – is-	• 阅读与评价该公司重大财务错报的可能性相关的公开资料，以及在整合审计中，与财务报告内部控制有效性相关的公开资料，比如，公司发表的公

sued press releases, company - prepared presentation materials for analysts or investor groups, and analyst reports;

报，公司为分析师或投资者团体编制的演示资料和分析报告；

• Observing or reading transcripts of earnings calls and, to the extent publicly available, other meetings with investors or rating agencies;

• 观察或阅读业绩电话会议的文稿以及其他可以公开获取的与投资者或评级机构召开的会议文稿；

• Obtaining an understanding of compensation arrangements with senior management, including incentive compensation arrangements, changes or adjustments to those arrangements, and special bonuses; and

• 了解与高级管理层相关的薪酬安排，包括激励性薪酬安排，对这些安排的变更或调整以及特殊奖金；和

• Obtaining information about trading activity in the company's securities and holdings in the company's securities by significant holders to identify potentially significant unusual developments (e.g., from Forms 3, 4, 5, 13D, and 13G).

• 获取该公司的证券交易活动资料和重大持股人的持股资料，以便识别潜在的重大异常进展（比如，从 Forms 3、4、5、13D 和 13G）。

Selection and Application of Accounting Principles, Including Related Disclosures

会计政策及其相关披露的选择和运用

12. As part of obtaining an understanding of the company's selection and application of accounting principles, including related disclosures, the auditor should evaluate whether the

12. 作为了解公司会计政策及其相关披露的选择和运用的一部分，审计师应当评价该公司会计政策的

company's selection and application of accounting principles are appropriate for its business and consistent with the applicable financial reporting framework and accounting principles used in the relevant industry. Also, to identify and assess risks of material misstatement related to omitted, incomplete, or inaccurate disclosures, the auditor should develop expectations about the disclosures that are necessary for the company's financial statements to be presented fairly in conformity with the applicable financial reporting framework.

选择和运用是否适合其经营，并且与适用的会计报告框架和相关行业所用的财务政策一致。另外，为了识别和评估与遗漏、不完整或不准确的披露有关的重大错报风险，审计师应当研究（财务报告使用者，译者注）对于披露的预期，这样的披露是遵照适用财务报告框架而公允披露的财务报表所必要的。

13. The following matters, if present, are relevant to the necessary understanding of the company's selection and application of accounting principles, including related disclosures:

13. 以下事项，如果发生，与所需了解公司会计政策及其相关披露的选择和运用有关：

• Significant changes in the company's accounting principles, financial reporting policies, or disclosures and the reasons for such changes;

• 公司会计政策 、财务报告政策或披露的重大变化及其理由；

• The financial reporting competencies of personnel involved in selecting and applying significant new or complex accounting principles;

• 选择和运用重大新的或复杂的会计政策的人员财务报告胜任能力；

- The accounts or disclosures for which judgment is used in the application of significant accounting principles, especially in determining management's estimates and assumptions;

- 在运用重大会计政策时，尤其是在确定管理层估计和假设时，需要运用判断的账户或披露；

- The effect of significant accounting principles in controversial or emerging areas for which there is a lack of authoritative guidance or consensus;

- 在缺乏权威的指引或一致意见的争议性领域或新领域中重大会计政策的影响；

- The methods the company uses to account for significant and unusual transactions; and

- 公司用于核算重大和非常规交易的方法；和

- Financial reporting standards and laws and regulations that are new to the company, including when and how the company will adopt such requirements.

- 对于公司而言新的财务报告准则和法律法规，包括公司何时和如何采用这些规定。

Company Objectives, Strategies, and Related Business Risks

公司目标、战略和相关经营风险

14. The purpose of obtaining an understanding of the company's objectives, strategies, and related business risks is to identify business risks that could reasonably be expected to result in material misstatement of the financial statements.

14. 了解公司目标、战略和相关经营风险的目的是识别那些可以被合理地预期将导致财务报表重大错报的经营风险。

Note: Some relevant business risks might be identified through other risk assessment procedures, such as obtaining an understanding of the nature of the company and understanding industry, regulatory, and other external factors.

注：某些相关经营风险可以通过其他风险评估程序识别，比如，通过了解公司的性质和行业、监管或其他外部因素。

15. The following are examples of situations in which business risks might result in material misstatement of the financial statements:

15. 以下是经营风险可能导致财务报告重大错报的情况举例：

- Industry developments (a potential related business risk might be, e. g. , that the company does not have the personnel or expertise to deal with the changes in the industry.)

- 行业发展（潜在的相关经营风险可能是公司没有人员或专门知识来应对行业变化。）

- New products and services (a potential related business risk might be, e. g. , that the new product or service will not be successful.)

- 新产品和服务（潜在的相关经营风险可能是新产品或服务不成功。）

- Use of information technology ("IT") (a potential related business risk might be, e. g. , that systems and processes are incompatible.)

- 信息技术（"IT"）的使用（潜在的相关经营风险可能是系统和流程不兼容。）

- New accounting requirements (a potential related business risk might be, e. g. , incomplete or improper implementation of a new accounting requirement.)

- 新的会计要求（潜在的相关经营风险可能是不完整或不适当地执行新的会计要求。）

• Expansion of the business (a potential related business risk might be, e. g. , that the demand for the company's products or services has not been accurately estimated.)

• 经营扩张（潜在的相关经营风险可能是没有准确估计对公司产品或服务的需求。）

• The effects of implementing a strategy, particularly any effects that will lead to new accounting requirements (a potential related business risk might be, e. g. , incomplete or improper implementation of the strategy.)

• 执行某战略的影响，尤其是导致新会计要求的影响（比如，潜在的相关经营风险可能是不完整或不适当地执行战略。）

• Current and prospective financing requirements (a potential related business risk might be, e. g. , the loss of financing due to the company's inability to meet financing requirements.)

• 当前或预期的融资需求（潜在的相关经营风险可能是由于公司未能满足融资要求而失去融资。）

• Regulatory requirements (a potential related business risk might be, e. g. , that there is increased legal exposure.)

• 监管要求（潜在的相关经营风险可能是更高的法律风险。）

Note: Business risks could affect risks of material misstatement at the financial statement level, which would affect many accounts and disclosures in the financial statements. For example, a company's loss of financing or declining conditions affecting the company's industry could affect its ability to settle its obligations when due. This, in turn, could affect the risks of material misstatement

注：经营风险可能影响财务报表层次的重大错报风险，涉及财务报表的众多账户和披露。例如，公司失去融资或影响公司所在行业的衰退可能影响其偿还负债。这反过来会影响与长期负债分类或长期资产估价有关的重大错报风

related to, e. g. , the classification of long-term liabilities or valuation of long-term assets, or it could result in substantial doubt about the company's ability to continue as a going concern. Other business risks could affect the risks of material misstatement for particular accounts, disclosures, or assertions. For example, an unsuccessful new product or service or failed business expansion might affect the risks of material misstatement related to the valuation of inventory and other related assets.

险，也可能导致对公司持续经营能力的严重质疑。其他经营风险可能导致特定账户、披露或认定的重大错报风险。例如，不成功的产品或服务，或者失败的经营扩张，可能影响与存货和其他相关资产的估价有关的重大错报风险。

Company Performance Measures

公司的业绩指标

16. The purpose of obtaining an understanding of the company's performance measures is to identify performance measures, whether external or internal, that affect the risks of material misstatement.

16. 了解公司的业绩指标的目的是识别影响重大错报风险的外部或内部的业绩指标。

17. The following are examples of performance measures that might affect the risks of material misstatement:

17. 以下是影响重大错报风险的业绩指标举例：

- Measures that form the basis for contractual commitments or incentive compensation arrangements;

- 构成契约性承诺或激励性薪酬安排的基础指标；

• Measures used by external parties, such as analysts and rating agencies, to review the company's performance; and

• 外部人员，比如分析师和评级机构，评价公司业绩的指标；和

• Measures the company uses to monitor its operations that highlight unexpected results or trends that prompt management to investigate their cause and take corrective action, including correction of misstatements.

• 公司用于监督其经营的指标，用于凸显非预期结果或趋势，提示管理层调查其原因，并采取纠正行动，包括纠正错报。

Note: The first two examples represent performance measures that can affect the risks of material misstatement by creating incentives or pressures for management of the company to manipulate certain accounts or disclosures to achieve certain performance targets (or conceal a failure to achieve those targets). The third example represents performance measures that management might use to monitor risks affecting the financial statements.

注：前两个例子代表业绩指标通过对公司管理层为了达成业绩目标（或隐瞒未达成目标）而操纵特定账户或披露产生激励或压力而影响重大错报风险。第三个例子代表管理层可以用来监控影响财务报表的风险的业绩指标。

Note: Smaller companies might have less formal processes to measure and review financial performance. In such cases, the auditor might identify relevant performance measures by considering the information that the company uses to manage the business.

注：较小的公司可以用不太正式的流程来计量和评价财务业绩。这时候，审计师应当通过审阅公司用来管理其经营的资料，识别相关的业绩指标。

Obtaining an Understanding of Internal Control Over Financial Reporting

了解财务报告内部控制

18. The auditor should obtain a sufficient understanding of each component[⑧] of internal control over financial reporting ("understanding of internal control") to (a) identify the types of potential misstatements, (b) assess the factors that affect the risks of material misstatement, and (c) design further audit procedures.

18. 审计师应当充分了解财务报告内部控制的各个组成部分（"了解内部控制"），以便（a）识别潜在错报的类型，（b）评估影响重大错报风险的因素，和（c）设计进一步审计程序。

19. The nature, timing, and extent of procedures that are necessary to obtain an understanding of internal control depend on the size and complexity of the company;[⑨] the auditor's existing knowledge of the company's internal control over financial reporting; the nature of the company's controls, including the company's use of IT; the nature and extent of changes in systems and operations; and the nature of the company's documentation of its internal control over financial reporting.

19. 了解内部控制所需程序的性质、时间和范围取决于公司的大小和复杂性；审计师对于公司财务报告内部控制的现有知识；公司控制的性质，包括公司对 IT 的运用；系统和经营变化的性质和范围；以及公司财务报告内部控制文档的性质。

Note: The auditor also might obtain an understanding of certain controls that are not part of internal control over financial repor-

注：审计师也可以了解某些不是财务报告内部控制的控制，比如，对于作为

ting, e. g. , controls over the completeness and accuracy of operating or other nonfinancial information used as audit evidence. [10]

审计证据的运营和其他非财务信息的完整性和准确性的控制。

20. Obtaining an understanding of internal control includes evaluating the design of controls that are relevant to the audit and determining whether the controls have been implemented.

20. 了解内部控制包括评价与审计有关的控制的设计以及确定这些控制是否被执行。

Note: Procedures the auditor performs to obtain evidence about design effectiveness include inquiry of appropriate personnel, observation of the company ' s operations , and inspection of relevant documentation. Walkthroughs, as described in paragraphs 37 – 38, that include these procedures ordinarily are sufficient to evaluate design effectiveness.

注：审计师实施的了解设计有效性的程序包括询问适当员工，观察公司的运营和审查有关文档。第 37 至 38 款描述的包括这些程序的穿行测试通常足以评价设计的有效性。

Note: Determining whether a control has been implemented means determining whether the control exists and whether the company is using it. The procedures to determine whether a control has been implemented may be performed in connection with the evaluation of its design. Procedures performed to determine whether a control has been implemented include inquiry of appropriate personnel, in combination with observation of the application of controls

注：确定控制是否被执行就是确定控制是否存在，而且，公司是否正在执行。确定控制是否被执行的程序可以与设计评价一起实施。确定控制是否被执行的程序包括询问适当员工，与观察控制的运用或审查文档相结合。第 37 至 38 款描述的包括这

or inspection of documentation. Walkthroughs, as described in paragraphs 37 – 38, that include these procedures ordinarily are sufficient to determine whether a control has been implemented.

些程序的穿行测试通常足以确定控制是否被执行。

21. Internal control over financial reporting can be described as consisting of the following components: [11]

21. 财务报告内部控制可以被描述为以下组成部分：

- The control environment,
- The company's risk assessment process,
- Information and communication,
- Control activities, and
- Monitoring of controls.

- 控制环境，
- 公司的风险评估过程，
- 信息和沟通，
- 控制活动，和
- 控制的监督

22. Management might use an internal control framework with components that differ from the components identified in the preceding paragraph when establishing and maintaining the company's internal control over financial reporting. In evaluating the design of controls and determining whether they have been implemented in an audit of financial statements only, the auditor may use the framework used by management or another suitable ,

22. 管理层在制定和保持公司的财务报告内部控制时可能采用与前款列举的组成部分不同的内部控制框架。在仅对财务报表的审计中评价控制的设计和确定其是否被执行时，审计师可以采用管理层使用的框架，或者，其他适宜的被认可的框架。对于整

recognized framework. [12] For integrated audits, Auditing Standard No. 5, states, "The auditor should use the same suitable, recognized control framework to perform his or her audit of internal control over financial reporting as management uses for its annual evaluation of the effectiveness of the company's internal control over financial reporting." [13] If the auditor uses a suitable, recognized internal control framework with components that differ from those listed in the preceding paragraph, the auditor should adapt the requirements in paragraphs 23 – 36 of this standard to conform to the components in the framework used.

合审计，审计准则第 5 号指出，"审计师应当采用与管理层用于公司财务报告内部控制年度评价相同的适宜的被认可的控制框架，实施财务报告内部控制审计。"如果审计师采用的适宜的被认可的内部控制框架的组成部分不同于上款所列，审计师应当调整本准则第 23 至 26 款的要求，以便符合其所采用的框架的组成部分。

Control Environment
控制环境

23. The auditor should obtain an understanding of the company's control environment, including the policies and actions of management, the board, and the audit committee concerning the company's control environment.

23. 审计师应当了解公司的控制环境，包括管理层、董事会和审计委员会有关公司控制环境采取的政策和行动。

24. Obtaining an understanding of the control environment includes assessing:

24. 了解控制环境包括评估：

- Whether management's philosophy and op-

- 管理层的理念和运营风

erating style promote effective internal control over financial reporting;

格是否提倡有效的财务报告内部控制；

• Whether sound integrity and ethical values, particularly of top management, are developed and understood; and

• 良好的诚信和道德价值观，尤其是最高管理层的，是否被制定和理解；和

• Whether the board or audit committee understands and exercises oversight responsibility over financial reporting and internal control.

• 董事会或审计委员会是否理解和履行财务报告和内部控制的监督责任。

Note: In an audit of financial statements only, this assessment may be based on the evidence obtained in understanding the control environment, in accordance with paragraph 23, and the other relevant knowledge possessed by the auditor. In an integrated audit of financial statements and internal control over financial reporting, Auditing Standard No. 5[14] describes the auditor's responsibility for evaluating the control environment.

注：当仅对财务报表审计时，该评估可以基于遵照第 23 款进行的在了解控制环境时获取的证据，以及审计师获取的其他知识。在财务报表和财务报告内部控制整合审计时，审计准则第 5 号描述了审计师对于评价控制环境的责任。

25. If the auditor identifies a control deficiency[15] in the company's control environment, the auditor should evaluate the extent to which this control deficiency is indicative of a fraud risk factor, as discussed in paragraphs 65 – 66 of this standard.

25. 如果审计师识别了公司控制环境的某个控制缺陷，审计师应当按照本准则第 65 至 66 款的论述，评价该控制缺陷所暗示的舞弊风险因素的范围。

The Company's Risk Assessment Process

公司的风险评估过程

26. The auditor should obtain an understanding of management's process for:

26. 审计师应当了解管理层对于以下事项的处理过程：

a. Identifying risks relevant to financial reporting objectives, including risks of material misstatement due to fraud ("fraud risks");

a. 识别与财务报告目标相关的风险，包括舞弊导致的重大错报风险（"舞弊风险"）；

b. Assessing the likelihood and significance of misstatements resulting from those risks; and

b. 评估这些风险导致的错报的可能性和重大性；和

c. Deciding about actions to address those risks.

c. 有关处理这些风险的行动的决定。

27. Obtaining an understanding of the company's risk assessment process includes obtaining an understanding of the risks of material misstatement identified and assessed by management and the actions taken to address those risks.

27. 了解公司的风险评估过程，包括管理层已识别和评定的重大错报风险，以及处理这些风险所采取的行动。

Information and Communication

信息和沟通

28. Information System Relevant to Financial

28. 与财务报告相关的信

Reporting. The auditor should obtain an understanding of the information system, including the related business processes, relevant to financial reporting, including:

息系统。审计师应当了解与财务报告有关的信息系统及其相关的经营过程，包括：

a. The classes of transactions in the company's operations that are significant to the financial statements;

a. 在公司运营中对于财务报表而言重大的交易类别；

b. The procedures, within both automated and manual systems, by which those transactions are initiated, authorized, processed, recorded, and reported;

b. 在自动和人工系统中，这些交易被发起、授权、处理、登记和报告的流程；

c. The related accounting records, supporting information, and specific accounts in the financial statements that are used to initiate, authorize, process, and record transactions;

c. 在财务报表中用于发起、授权、处理和登记交易的相关会计记录、支持性资料和特定账户；

d. How the information system captures events and conditions, other than transactions, [16] that are significant to the financial statements; and

d. 信息系统如何捕捉交易之外的对于财务报表而言重大的事件和状况；和

e. The period - end financial reporting process.

e. 期末财务报告过程。

Note: Appendix B discusses additional considerations regarding manual and automated systems and controls.

注：附录 B 讨论关于人工和自动系统及控制的进一步考虑。

29. The auditor also should obtain an understanding of how IT affects the company's flow of transactions. (See Appendix B.)

29. 审计师也应当了解IT如何影响公司的交易流。(参见附录B。)

Note: The identification of risks and controls within IT is not a separate evaluation. Instead, it is an integral part of the approach used to identify significant accounts and disclosures and their relevant assertions and, when applicable, to select the controls to test, as well as to assess risk and allocate audit effort.

注：对于IT风险和控制的识别不是一个单独的评价。正相反，它不仅是用于识别账户和披露及其相关认定的方法不可分割的一部分，而且，如果适用，还是选择受测控制和评估风险、分配审计资源的方法不可分割的一部分。

30. A company's business processes are the activities designed to:

30. 公司经营过程是为以下目的设计的活动：

a. Develop, purchase, produce, sell and distribute a company's products or services;

a. 开发、采购、生产、销售和配送公司的产品或服务；

b. Record information, including accounting and financial reporting information; and

b. 登记资料，包括会计和财务报告资料；和

c. Ensure compliance with laws and regulations relevant to the financial statements.

c. 确保遵守与财务报表相关的法律和法规。

31. Obtaining an understanding of the company's business processes assists the auditor in obtaining an understanding of how transac-

31. 了解公司的经营过程帮助审计师了解交易如何被发起、授权、处理和登

tions are initiated, authorized, processed, and recorded.

记。

32. A company's period – end financial reporting process, as referred to in paragraph 28. e. , includes the following:

32. 第28. e 款提及的公司期末财务报告过程包括：

• Procedures used to enter transaction totals into the general ledger;

• 将交易合计过入总分类账的流程；

• Procedures related to the selection and application of accounting principles; [17]

与会计政策的选择和运用有关的流程；

• Procedures used to initiate, authorize, record, and process journal entries in the general ledger;

• 在总分类账中发起、授权、登记和处理分录的流程；

• Procedures used to record recurring and nonrecurring adjustments to the annual financial statements (and quarterly financial statements, if applicable); and

• 在年度财务报表（和季度财务报表，如果适用的话）中登记经常性和非经常性调整的流程；和

• Procedures for preparing annual financial statements and related disclosures (and quarterly financial statements, if applicable).

• 编制年度财务报表（和季度财务报表，如果适用的话）和相关披露的流程。

33. Communication. The auditor should obtain an understanding of how the company communicates financial reporting roles and responsibilities and significant matters rela-

33. 沟通。审计师应当了解公司如何将其财务报告角色和责任以及与财务报告相关的重大事项，与相

ting to financial reporting to relevant company personnel and others, including:

关公司人员和其他人员沟通，包括：

- Communications between management, the audit committee, and the board of directors; and

- 与管理层、审计委员会和董事会沟通；和

- Communications to external parties, including regulatory authorities and shareholders.

- 与外部人员沟通，包括监管机构和股东。

Control Activities
控制活动

34. The auditor should obtain an understanding of control activities that is sufficient to assess the factors that affect the risks of material misstatement and to design further audit procedures, as described in paragraph 18 of this standard. [18] As the auditor obtains an understanding of the other components of internal control over financial reporting, he or she is also likely to obtain knowledge about some control activities. The auditor should use his or her knowledge about the presence or absence of control activities obtained from the understanding of the other components of internal control over financial reporting in determining the extent to which it is necessary to devote additional attention to obtaining an understanding of control activities to assess the factors that affect the risks of material misstatement and to design

34. 审计师应当按照本准则第 18 款描述的那样，了解控制活动，以便充分地评估影响重大错报的风险因素，并且设计进一步的审计程序。当审计师了解财务报告内部控制的其他组成部分的时候，也有可能获得控制活动方面的知识。审计师应当利用其对于其他财务报告内部控制组成部分的了解，知道控制活动存在与否，从而确定给予更多关注来了解控制活动所需的范围，以便评估影响重大错报风险的因素，并设计进一步审计程序。

further audit procedures.

Note: A broader understanding of control activities is needed for relevant assertions for which the auditor plans to rely on controls. Also, in the audit of internal control over financial reporting, the auditor's understanding of control activities encompasses a broader range of accounts and disclosures than what is normally obtained in a financial statement audit.

注：对于那些审计师计划依赖于控制的相关认定，需要对控制活动有更宽泛的了解。另外，在财务报告内部控制审计中，审计师了解控制活动涵盖的账户和披露的范围通常要大于财务报表审计。

Monitoring of Controls
控制的监督

35. The auditor should obtain an understanding of the major types of activities that the company uses to monitor the effectiveness of its internal control over financial reporting and how the company initiates corrective actions related to its controls. [19]

35. 审计师应当了解公司用来监督财务报告内部控制有效性的活动的主要类型，以及公司如何启动与这些控制相关的纠正行动。

36. An understanding of the company's monitoring activities includes understanding the source of the information used in the monitoring activities.

36. 了解公司的监控活动包括了解用于监控活动的信息来源。

Performing Walkthroughs
执行穿行测试

37. As discussed in paragraph 20, the audi-

37. 如同第 20 款讨论的，

tor may perform walkthroughs as part of obtaining an understanding of internal control over financial reporting. For example, the auditor may perform walkthroughs in connection with understanding the flow of transactions in the information system relevant to financial reporting, evaluating the design of controls relevant to the audit, and determining whether those controls have been implemented . In performing a walkthrough , the auditor follows a transaction from origination through the company's processes, including information systems, until it is reflected in the company's financial records, using the same documents and IT that company personnel use. Walkthrough procedures usually include a combination of inquiry, observation, inspection of relevant documentation, and re – performance of controls.

审计师可以实施穿行测试，作为了解财务报告内部控制的一部分。例如，审计师可以在了解与财务报告相关的信息系统交易流时实施穿行测试，并确定这些控制是否被执行。在实施穿行测试时，审计师利用与公司员工相同的文档，随着交易从源头走过公司的流程，包括信息系统，直至其反映到公司的财务记录。穿行测试程序通常包括询问、观察、审阅相关文档和控制的重新运行。

Note: For integrated audits, Auditing Standard No. 5 establishes certain objectives that the auditor should achieve to further understand likely sources of potential misstatements and as part of selecting the controls to test. Auditing Standard No. 5 states that performing walkthroughs will frequently be the most effective way of achieving those objectives. [20]

注：对于整合审计，审计准则第 5 号制定了审计师为了进一步了解潜在错报的来源，以及作为选择受测控制的一部分，应当达成的特定目标。审计准则第 5 号指出实施穿行测试通常是达成这些目标最有效的办法。

38. In performing a walkthrough, at the points at which important processing procedures occur, the auditor questions the company's personnel about their understanding of what is required by the company's prescribed procedures and controls. These probing questions, combined with the other walkthrough procedures, allow the auditor to gain a sufficient understanding of the process and to be able to identify important points at which a necessary control is missing or not designed effectively. Additionally, probing questions that go beyond a narrow focus on the single transaction used as the basis for the walkthrough allow the auditor to gain an understanding of the different types of significant transactions handled by the process.

38. 实施穿行测试时，在发生重要处理程序的节点上，审计师询问公司员工对于公司既定程序和控制的了解。这些深入的问题与其他穿行测试程序一起，可以使审计师充分了解该过程，并能够识别那些缺失必要的控制或控制未能有效设计的重要节点。另外，超出仅限于单个交易的穿行测试而提出的深入性问题，可以使审计师了解该过程所处理的不同类型的重大交易。

Relationship of Understanding of Internal Control to Tests of Controls

了解内部控制与控制测试的关系

39. The objective of obtaining an understanding of internal control, as discussed in paragraph 18 of this standard, is different from testing controls for the purpose of assessing control risk[21] or for the purpose of expressing an opinion on internal control over financial reporting in the audit of internal control over financial reporting.[22] The auditor may obtain

39. 本准则第 18 款讨论的了解内部控制的目的与为了评估控制风险所做的控制测试不同，也与财务报告内部控制审计中为了对财务报告内部控制发表意见所做的控制测试不同。审计师可以在了解内

an understanding of internal control concurrently with performing tests of controls if he or she obtains sufficient appropriate evidence to achieve the objectives of both procedures. Also, the auditor should take into account the evidence obtained from understanding internal control when assessing control risk and, in the audit of internal control over financial reporting, forming an opinion about the effectiveness of internal control over financial reporting.

部控制的同时，实施控制测试，只要审计师取得了完成两个程序所需的充分适当的证据。另外，审计师应当将评估控制风险时了解内部控制获取的证据考虑在内，以及将在财务报告内部控制审计中形成财务报告内部控制有效性的意见时获取的证据考虑在内。

40. Relationship of Understanding of Internal Control to Evaluating Entity – Level Controls in an Audit of Internal Control Over Financial Reporting. Auditing Standard No. 5 states, "The auditor must test those entity – level controls that are important to the auditor's conclusion about whether the company has effective internal control over financial reporting." ㉓ The procedures performed to obtain an understanding of certain components of internal control in accordance with this standard, e. g. , the control environment, the company's risk assessment process, information and communication, and monitoring of controls, might provide evidence that is relevant to the auditor's evaluation of entity – level controls. ㉔ The auditor should take into account the evidence ob-

40. 在财务报告内部控制审计中了解内部控制与评价实体层面控制的关系。审计准则第 5 号指出"审计师必须测试对于审计师有关公司是否具备有效的财务报告内部控制的结论而言重要的实体层面控制。"按照本准则的要求实施的程序所了解到的内部控制的某些组成部分，比如，控制环境、公司的风险评估过程、信息和沟通以及控制的监督，可能为审计师实体层面控制的评价提供证据。在财务报告内部控制审计中，当确定支持审计师有关实体层

tained from understanding internal control when determining the nature, timing, and extent of procedures necessary to support the auditor's conclusions about the effectiveness of entity – level controls in the audit of internal control over financial reporting.

面控制的有效性所需程序的性质、时间和范围时，审计师应当将在了解内部控制时所获证据考虑在内。

Considering Information from the Client Acceptance and Retention Evaluation, Audit Planning Activities, Past Audits, and Other Engagements

考虑接纳和保留客户的评价、审计计划活动、以往审计和其他业务中取得的资料

41. Client Acceptance and Retention and Audit Planning Activities. The auditor should evaluate whether information obtained from the client acceptance and retention evaluation process or audit planning activities is relevant to identifying risks of material misstatement. Risks of material misstatement identified during those activities should be assessed as discussed beginning in paragraph 59 of this standard.

41. 接纳和保留客户以及审计计划活动。审计师应当考虑接纳和保留客户的评价或者审计计划活动中所获取的资料是否与识别重大错报风险相关。应当按照本准则第 59 款开始的讨论那样评估在这些活动中识别的重大错报风险。

42. Past Audits. In subsequent years, the auditor should incorporate knowledge obtained during past audits into the auditor's process for identifying risks of material misstatement, including when identifying significant ongo-

42. 以往审计。在后续年度，审计师应当将以往审计获得的知识吸收到识别重大错报风险的过程中，包括识别影响重大错报风

ing matters that affect the risks of material misstatement or determining how changes in the company or its environment affect the risks of material misstatement, as discussed in paragraph 8 of this standard.

险的正在发生的重大事项，或者，如同本准则第 8 款所讨论的，确定公司及其环境的改变如何影响重大错报风险。

43. If the auditor plans to limit the nature, timing, or extent of his or her risk assessment procedures by relying on information from past audits, the auditor should evaluate whether the prior years' information remains relevant and reliable.

43. 如果审计师计划依赖以往审计的资料限定其风险评估程序的性质、时间和范围，审计师应当评价以往年度的资料是否仍然相关和可靠。

44. Other Engagements. When the auditor has performed a review of interim financial information in accordance with AU sec. 722, Interim Financial Information, the auditor should evaluate whether information obtained during the review is relevant to identifying risks of material misstatement in the year-end audit.

44. 其他业务。当审计师已经遵照过渡性审计准则第 722 条［中期财务资料］实施了中期财务资料审阅，审计师应当评价在该审阅中获得的资料是否与在年末审计中识别重大错报风险相关。

45. The auditor should obtain an understanding of the nature of the services that have been performed for the company by the auditor or affiliates of the firm[25] and should take into account relevant information obtained from those engagements in identifying risks of material misstatement.[26]

45. 审计师应当了解事务所的成员所或其审计师所提供服务的性质，并在识别重大错报风险时将从这些业务中所获得的相关资料考虑在内。

Performing Analytical Procedures
实施分析性程序

46. The auditor should perform analytical procedures that are designed to:

46. 审计师应当实施分析性程序，用于：

a. Enhance the auditor's understanding of the client's business and the significant transactions and events that have occurred since the prior year end; and

a. 提高审计师对于上年度结束以来客户发生的经营、重大交易和事件的了解；和

b. Identify areas that might represent specific risks relevant to the audit, including the existence of unusual transactions and events, and amounts, ratios, and trends that warrant investigation.

b. 识别可能表明与审计相关的特定风险领域，包括存在需要调查的非正常交易和事件、金额、比率和趋势。

47. In applying analytical procedures as risk assessment procedures, the auditor should perform analytical procedures relating to revenue with the objective of identifying unusual or unexpected relationships involving revenue accounts that might indicate a material misstatement, including material misstatement due to fraud. Also, when the auditor has performed a review of interim financial information in accordance with AU sec. 722, he or she should take into account the analytical procedures applied in that review when designing and applying analytical procedures as

47. 在应用分析性复核程序作为风险评估程序时，审计师应当实施与收入有关的分析性复核程序，目的是识别可能表示重大错报风险（包括舞弊导致的重大错报）的非正常或非预期的涉及收入帐户的关系。另外，当审计师已经遵照过渡性审计准则第722条实施了中期财务资料审阅，那么，审计师应当在设计和应用分析性程

risk assessment procedures.

序作为风险评估程序时，将在该审阅中实施的分析性复核程序考虑在内。

48. When performing an analytical procedure, the auditor should use his or her understanding of the company to develop expectations about plausible relationships among the data to be used in the procedure. [27] When comparison of those expectations with relationships derived from recorded amounts yields unusual or unexpected results, the auditor should take into account those results in identifying the risks of material misstatement.

48. 当实施分析性程序时，审计师应当利用对公司的了解，提出用于该程序的这些数据之间应有关系的预期。当账面金额得出的关系与这些预期相比较出现非正常或非预期的结果，审计师应当在识别重大错报风险时将这些结果考虑在内。

Note: Analytical procedures performed as risk assessment procedures often use data that is preliminary or data that is aggregated at a high level, and, in those instances, such analytical procedures are not designed with the level of precision necessary for substantive analytical procedures.

注：用作风险评估程序的分析性程序通常利用初步数据或在高层次合计的数据，此时，这些分析性程序不是设计成实质性分析程序所需的准确程度。

Conducting a Discussion among Engagement Team Members Regarding Risks of Material Misstatement

就重大错报风险在业务团队成员间讨论

49. The key engagement team members should

49. 业务团队的关键成员

discuss (1) the company's selection and application of accounting principles, including related disclosure requirements, and (2) the susceptibility of the company's financial statements to material misstatement due to error or fraud.

应当讨论（1）公司对于会计政策的选择和运用，包括相关披露要求，和（2）由于错误或舞弊造成公司财务报表重大错报的敏感性。

Note: The key engagement team members should discuss the potential for material misstatement due to fraud either as part of the discussion regarding risks of material misstatement or in a separate discussion. ㉘

注：业务团队的关键成员应当讨论舞弊造成的重大错报的可能性，要么作为重大错报风险讨论的一部分，要么作为分开的讨论。

Note: As discussed in paragraph 67, the financial statements might be susceptible to misstatement through omission of required disclosures or presentation of inaccurate or incomplete disclosures.

注：如同第 67 款讨论的，财务报表可能由于缺少规定的披露或者列报不准确或不完整的披露，而容易被错报。

50. Key engagement team members include all engagement team members who have significant engagement responsibilities, including the engagement partner. The manner in which the discussion is conducted depends on the individuals involved and the circumstances of the engagement. For example, if the audit involves more than one location, there could be multiple discussions with team members in differing locations. The engagement partner or other key engagement team

50. 业务团队的关键成员包括所有承担重大业务责任的业务团队成员，包括业务合伙人。讨论采取的方式取决于涉及的人员和业务的情况。例如，如果审计涉及一个以上的场所，团队成员可以在不同的场所开展多次讨论。业务合伙人或业务团队的其他关键成员应当向没有参

members should communicate the important matters from the discussion to engagement team members who are not involved in the discussion.

与讨论的业务团队成员传达讨论的重要事项。

Note: If the audit is performed entirely by the engagement partner, that engagement partner, having personally conducted the planning of the audit, is responsible for evaluating the susceptibility of the company's financial statements to material misstatement.

注：如果审计完全由业务合伙人实施，那么，亲自实施审计计划的业务合伙人负责评价公司财务报表重大错报的敏感性。

51. Communication among the engagement team members about significant matters affecting the risks of material misstatement should continue throughout the audit, including when conditions change. ㉙

51. 应当在审计中持续地在业务团队成员之间传达影响重大错报风险的重大事项，包括状况发生变化时。

Discussion of the Potential for Material Misstatement Due to Fraud

讨论舞弊造成的潜在重大错报

52. The discussion among the key engagement team members about the potential for material misstatement due to fraud should occur with an attitude that includes a questioning mind, and the key engagement team members should set aside any prior beliefs they might have that management is honest and has integrity. The discussion among the

52. 业务团队关键成员之间有关舞弊造成潜在重大错报的讨论应当以质疑的态度进行，并且，业务团队关键成员应当将以前认为其管理层是诚实和诚信的想法放到一边。在业务团队关键成员之间的讨论

key engagement team members should include:

包括：

• An exchange of ideas, or "brainstorming," among the key engagement team members, including the engagement partner, about how and where they believe the company's financial statements might be susceptible to material misstatement due to fraud, how management could perpetrate and conceal fraudulent financial reporting, and how assets of the company could be misappropriated, including (a) the susceptibility of the financial statements to material misstatement through related party transactions and (b) how fraud might be perpetrated or concealed by omitting or presenting incomplete or inaccurate disclosures;

• 在业务团队关键成员之间，包括业务合伙人，就公司财务报表如何和哪里存在舞弊造成的重大错报的敏感性、管理层如何提交并掩盖舞弊性财务报告，以及公司资产如何被挪用，交换意见或者“头脑风暴”，包括（1）通过关联方交易造成的公司财务报表重大错报的敏感性和（b）如何通过遗漏或提交不完整或不准确的披露而产生或掩盖舞弊行为；

• A consideration of the known external and internal factors affecting the company that might (a) create incentives or pressures for management and others to commit fraud, (b) provide the opportunity for fraud to be perpetrated, and (c) indicate a culture or environment that enables management to rationalize committing fraud;

• 考虑已知的影响公司的外部和内部因素，例如（a）催生管理层或他人舞弊的诱因或压力，（b）提供发生舞弊的机会，和（c）使得管理层认为舞弊合理的文化或环境；

• A consideration of the risk of management override; and

• 对于管理层越权的考虑；和

• A consideration of the potential audit responses to the susceptibility of the company's financial statements to material misstatement due to fraud.

• 对于公司财务报表存在舞弊造成的重大错报的敏感性而采取的潜在审计应对策略的考虑。

53. The auditor should emphasize the following matters to all engagement team members:

53. 审计师应当向全体业务团队成员强调以下事项:

• The need to maintain a questioning mind throughout the audit and to exercise professional skepticism in gathering and evaluating evidence, as described in AU sec. 316; [30]

• 需要在审计全过程保持质疑的心态，并按照过渡性审计准则第 316 条的规定，在收集和评价证据时秉持职业怀疑态度;

• The need to be alert for information or other conditions (such as those matters presented in Appendix C of Auditing Standard No. 14) that might affect the assessment of fraud risks; and

• 需要对可能影响舞弊风险评估的信息或其他状况保持警觉（比如在审计准则第 14 号附录 C 列举的那些事项）; 和

• If information or other conditions indicate that a material misstatement due to fraud might have occurred, the need to probe the issues, acquire additional evidence as necessary, and consult with other team members and, if appropriate, others in the firm including specialists. [31]

• 如果信息或其他状况表明已经发生了舞弊造成的重大错报，是否需要深入研究该事项、取得必要的进一步证据、咨询其他团队成员和（如果适当的话）事务所的其他人员（包括专家）。

Inquiring of the Audit Committee, Management, and Others within the Company about the Risks of Material Misstatement
就重大错报风险询问审计委员会、管理层和公司中的其他人员

54. The auditor should inquire of the audit committee, or equivalent (or its chair), management, the internal audit function, and others within the company who might reasonably be expected to have information that is important to the identification and assessment of risks of material misstatement.

54. 审计师应当询问审计委员会或与之等同的（或其主席）、管理层、内部审计部门和公司中其他可以被合理地认为了解识别和评估重大错报风险重要信息的人员。

Note: The auditor's inquiries about risks of material misstatement should include inquiries regarding fraud risks.

注：审计师有关重大错报风险的询问应当包括与舞弊风险有关的询问。

55. The auditor should use his or her knowledge of the company and its environment, as well as information from other risk assessment procedures, to determine the nature of the inquiries about risks of material misstatement.

55. 审计师应当利用对公司及其环境的了解，以及其他风险评估程序获得的资料，确定对于重大错报风险询问的性质。

Inquiries Regarding Fraud Risks
询问舞弊风险

56. The auditor's inquiries regarding fraud

56. 审计师询问舞弊风险

risks should include the following:

应当包括：

a. Inquiries of management regarding:

a. 询问管理层：

(1) Whether management has knowledge of fraud, alleged fraud, or suspected fraud affecting the company;

(1) 管理层是否具有舞弊知识、了解被告发的舞弊或影响公司的可疑舞弊；

(2) Management's process for identifying and responding to fraud risks in the company, including any specific fraud risks the company has identified or account balances or disclosures for which a fraud risk is likely to exist, and the nature, extent, and frequency of management's fraud risk assessment process;

(2) 管理层用于识别和应对公司中舞弊风险的过程，包括公司识别的任何特定舞弊风险，或者，可能存在舞弊风险的账户余额或披露，以及管理层的舞弊风险评估过程的性质、范围和频率；

(3) Controls that the company has established to address fraud risks the company has identified, or that otherwise help to prevent and detect fraud, including how management monitors those controls;

(3) 公司建立的处理已识别的舞弊风险的控制，或者，帮助防范和发现舞弊的控制，包括公司如何监督这些控制；

(4) For a company with multiple locations (a) the nature and extent of monitoring of operating locations or business segments and (b) whether there are particular operating locations or business segments for which a fraud risk might be more likely to exist;

(4) 对于多场所的公司 (a) 经营场所或业务单元监控的性质和范围，以及 (b) 是否存在较易发生舞弊风险的个别场所或业务单元；

(5) Whether and how management communicates to employees its views on business practices and ethical behavior;

（5）管理层是否和如何向员工传达其对于经营实践和其他行为的看法；

(6) Whether management has received tips or complaints regarding the company's financial reporting (including those received through the audit committee's internal whistleblower program, if such program exists) and, if so, management's responses to such tips and complaints; and

（6）管理层是否收到与公司财务报告有关的举报或投诉（包括那些通过审计委员会的内部举报机制收到的，如果该机制存在的话），以及，管理层对于这些线索和抱怨的回应；和

(7) Whether management has reported to the audit committee on how the company's internal control serves to prevent and detect material misstatements due to fraud.

（7）管理层是否已向审计委员会报告公司的内部控制如何防范和发现舞弊导致的重大错报。

b. Inquiries of the audit committee, or equivalent, or its chair regarding:

b. 询问审计委员会或其主席：

(1) The audit committee's views about fraud risks in the company;

（1）审计委员会对于公司舞弊风险的看法；

(2) Whether the audit committee has knowledge of fraud, alleged fraud, or suspected fraud affecting the company;

（2）审计委员会是否具有舞弊知识，了解被告发的舞弊或影响公司的可疑舞弊；

(3) Whether the audit committee is aware of tips or complaints regarding the company's

（3）审计委员会是否知悉与公司财务报告有关的

financial reporting (including those received through the audit committee's internal whistleblower program, if such program exists) and, if so, the audit committee's responses to such tips and complaints; and

举报或投诉（包括那些通过审计委员会的内部举报机制收到的，如果该机制存在的话），以及，审计委员会对于这些举报和投诉的答复；和

(4) How the audit committee exercises oversight of the company's assessment of fraud risks and the establishment of controls to address fraud risks.

(4) 审计委员会如何监督公司舞弊风险的评估，以及为处理舞弊风险建立控制。

c. If the company has an internal audit function, inquiries of appropriate internal audit personnel regarding:

c. 如果公司有内部审计部门，询问适当的内部审计人员：

(1) The internal auditors' views about fraud risks in the company;

(1) 内部审计师对于公司舞弊风险的看法；

(2) Whether the internal auditors have knowledge of fraud, alleged fraud, or suspected fraud affecting the company;

(2) 内部审计师是否具有舞弊知识，了解被告发的舞弊或影响公司的可疑舞弊；

(3) Whether internal auditors have performed procedures to identify or detect fraud during the year, and whether management has satisfactorily responded to the findings resulting from those procedures; and

(3) 内部审计师是否在本年已经实施了程序识别或发现舞弊，而且，管理层是否对这些程序的发现结果做出了令人满意的答复；和

(4) Whether internal auditors are aware of instances of management override of controls and the nature and circumstances of such overrides.

（4）内部审计师是否知道管理层凌驾于控制之上的事件及其性质和具体情况。

57. In addition to the inquiries outlined in the preceding paragraph, the auditor should inquire of others within the company about their views regarding fraud risks, including, in particular, whether they have knowledge of fraud, alleged fraud, or suspected fraud. The auditor should identify other individuals within the company to whom inquiries should be directed and determine the extent of such inquiries by considering whether others in the company might have additional knowledge about fraud, alleged fraud, or suspected fraud or might be able to corroborate fraud risks identified in discussions with management or the audit committee. Examples of other individuals within the company to whom inquiries might be directed include:

57. 在上款列举的询问之外，审计师应当询问公司中的其他人员对于舞弊风险的看法，尤其包括他们是否具有舞弊知识、了解被告发的舞弊或可疑舞弊。审计师应当识别公司内应当询问的人员，并通过考虑这些人员是否了解更多的有关舞弊、被告发的舞弊或可疑舞弊的情况，确定询问的范围，或者，可以与在管理层或审计委员会讨论中识别的舞弊风险相互印证。公司中可以询问的其他人员包括：

• Employees with varying levels of authority within the company, including, e. g., company personnel with whom the auditor comes into contact during the course of the audit (a) in obtaining an understanding of internal control, (b) in observing inventory or performing cutoff procedures, or (c) in obtaining explanations for significant differences i-

• 公司中有不同层次权限的员工，包括，审计师在审计中为了（a）了解内部控制，（b）观察存货或者实施会计截止程序，或（c）了解实施分析性程序识别的重大差异，所接触的公司员工；

dentified when performing analytical procedures;

• Operating personnel not directly involved in the financial reporting process;

• 不直接参与财务报告过程的运营人员；

• Employees involved in initiating, recording, or processing complex or unusual transactions, e. g. , a sales transaction with multiple elements or a significant related party transaction; and

• 参与发起、登记或处理复杂或非常规交易的员工，比如，有多重要素的销售交易，或者重大关联方交易；和

• In – house legal counsel.

• 内部法律顾问。

58. When evaluating management's responses to inquiries about fraud risks and determining when it is necessary to corroborate management's responses, the auditor should take into account the fact that management is often in the best position to commit fraud. Also, the auditor should obtain evidence to address inconsistencies in responses to the inquiries.

58. 在评价管理层对于舞弊风险询问的回复和确定何时需要与管理层的回复印证时,审计师应当将管理层总是处于产生舞弊行为的最佳位置考虑在内。另外,审计师应当获取证据,解决对询问的不一致回答。

Identifying and Assessing the Risks of Material Misstatement

识别和评估重大错报风险

59. The auditor should identify and assess the risks of material misstatement at the financial statement level and the assertion level. In identifying and assessing risks of material

59. 审计师应当识别和评估财务报表层次和认定层次的重大错报风险。在识别和评估重大错报风险

misstatement, the auditor should:

时，审计师应当：

a. Identify risks of misstatement using information obtained from performing risk assessment procedures (as discussed in paragraphs 4 – 58) and considering the characteristics of the accounts and disclosures in the financial statements.

a. 利用实施风险评估程序获得的资料识别错报风险（如第 4 至 48 款所讨论的）并且考虑财务报表账户和披露的特点。

Note: Factors relevant to identifying fraud risks are discussed in paragraphs 65 – 69 of this standard.

注：与识别舞弊风险相关的因素在本准则第 65 至 69 款讨论。

b. Evaluate whether the identified risks relate pervasively to the financial statements as a whole and potentially affect many assertions.

b. 评价已识别风险是否广泛地与财务报表整体有关，而且潜在地影响众多认定。

c. Evaluate the types of potential misstatements that could result from the identified risks and the accounts, disclosures, and assertions that could be affected.

c. 评价已识别风险可能造成的潜在错报的类型，以及可能影响的账户、披露和认定。

Note: In identifying and assessing risks at the assertion level, the auditor should evaluate how risks at the financial statement level could affect risks of misstatement at the assertion level.

注：在识别和评估认定层次风险时，审计师应当评价财务报表层次的风险如何影响认定层次的错报风险。

d. Assess the likelihood of misstatement, including the possibility of multiple misstate-

d. 评估错报的可能性，包括多重错报的可能性，

ments, and the magnitude of potential misstatement to assess the possibility that the risk could result in material misstatement of the financial statements.

以及潜在错报的严重性，以便评估可能导致财务报表重大错报的风险。

Note: In assessing the likelihood and magnitude of potential misstatement, the auditor may take into account the planned degree of reliance on controls selected to test. [32]

注：在评估潜在错报的可能性和严重性时，审计师可以将对于被测控制的预定信赖程度考虑在内。

e. Identify significant accounts and disclosures [33] and their relevant assertions [34] (paragraphs 60 – 64 of this standard).

e. 识别重要账户和披露及其相关认定（本准则第 60 至 64 款）。

Note: The determination of whether an account or disclosure is significant or whether an assertion is a relevant assertion is based on inherent risk, without regard to the effect of controls.

注：确定某个账户或披露是否重大，或者某个认定是否相关认定，是基于固有风险，而不论控制的影响。

f. Determine whether any of the identified and assessed risks of material misstatement are significant risks (paragraphs 70 – 71 of this standard).

f. 确定已识别和评定的重大错报风险是否为重大风险（本准则第 70 至 71 款）

Identifying Significant Accounts and Disclosures and Their Relevant Assertions

识别重要账户和披露及其相关认定

60. To identify significant accounts and disclosures and their relevant assertions in ac-

60. 为了遵照第 59. e. 款识别重要账户和披露及其

cordance with paragraph 59. e. , the auditor should evaluate the qualitative and quantitative risk factors related to the financial statement line items and disclosures. Risk factors relevant to the identification of significant accounts and disclosures and their relevant assertions include:

相关认定，审计师应当评价与财务报表项目和披露有关的质和量的风险因素。与识别重要账户和披露及其相关认定有关的风险因素包括：

- Size and composition of the account;

- 账户的大小和组成；

- Susceptibility to misstatement due to error or fraud;

- 错报对于错误或舞弊的敏感性；

- Volume of activity, complexity, and homogeneity of the individual transactions processed through the account or reflected in the disclosure;

- 经该账户处理或该披露反映的个别交易的数量、复杂性和同质性；

- Nature of the account or disclosure;

- 账户或披露的性质；

- Accounting and reporting complexities associated with the account or disclosure;

- 与账户或披露相关的会计和报告的复杂性；

- Exposure to losses in the account;

- 该账户发生亏损的风险；

- Possibility of significant contingent liabilities arising from the activities reflected in the account or disclosure;

- 该帐户或披露反映的活动导致的重大或有负债的可能性；

- Existence of related party transactions in the account; and

- 该账户存在关联方交易；和

- Changes from the prior period in account and disclosure characteristics.

- 账户和披露的特点与前期发生变化。

61. As part of identifying significant accounts and disclosures and their relevant assertions, the auditor also should determine the likely sources of potential misstatements that would cause the financial statements to be materially misstated. The auditor might determine the likely sources of potential misstatements by asking himself or herself "what could go wrong?" within a given significant account or disclosure.

61. 作为识别重要账户和披露及其相关认定的一部分，审计师还应当确定可能导致财务报表重大错报的潜在错报的可能来源。审计师可以通过自问“什么会出错”来确定给定重要账户或披露的潜在错报的可能来源。

62. The risk factors that the auditor should evaluate in the identification of significant accounts and disclosures and their relevant assertions are the same in the audit of internal control over financial reporting as in the audit of the financial statements; accordingly, significant accounts and disclosures and their relevant assertions are the same for both audits.

62. 财务报告内部控制审计中审计师在识别重要账户和披露及其相关认定所考虑的风险因素与财务报表审计是相同的；因此，对于二者而言，重要账户和披露及其相关认定是相同的。

Note: In the financial statement audit, the auditor might perform substantive auditing procedures on financial statement accounts, disclosures, and assertions that are not deter-

注：在财务报表审计中，审计师可以对没有确定为重要账户和披露及其相关认定的那些财务报表账户

mined to be significant accounts and disclosures and relevant assertions. [35]

和披露及其相关认定实施实质性审计程序。

63. The components of a potential significant account or disclosure might be subject to significantly differing risks.

63. 潜在的重要账户或披露的组成部分可能面临显著不同的风险。

64. When a company has multiple locations or business units, the auditor should identify significant accounts and disclosures and their relevant assertions based on the consolidated financial statements.

64. 当公司有多个场所或业务单元时，审计师应当基于合并财务报表识别重要账户和披露及其相关认定。

Factors Relevant to Identifying Fraud Risks
与识别舞弊风险有关的因素

65. The auditor should evaluate whether the information gathered from the risk assessment procedures indicates that one or more fraud risk factors are present and should be taken into account in identifying and assessing fraud risks. Fraud risk factors are events or conditions that indicate (1) an incentive or pressure to perpetrate fraud, (2) an opportunity to carry out the fraud, or (3) an attitude or rationalization that justifies the fraudulent action. Fraud risk factors do not necessarily indicate the existence of fraud; however, they often are present in circumstances in which fraud exists . Examples of fraud risk

65. 审计师应当评价风险评估程序收集的资料是否表明出现一个或多个舞弊风险因素，而且，应当在识别和评估舞弊风险时将其考虑在内。舞弊风险因素是暗示以下情形的事件或状况：（1）舞弊的诱因或压力，（2）舞弊的机会，或（3）为舞弊行为辩护的态度或借口。舞弊风险因素不表示必然存在舞弊；但是，发生舞弊时通常都存在舞弊风险因

factors related to fraudulent financial reporting and misappropriation of assets are listed in AU sec. 316. 85. These illustrative risk factors are classified based on the three conditions discussed in this paragraph, which generally are present when fraud exists.

素。过渡性审计准则第316. 85条列举了与舞弊性财务报告和挪用资产有关的舞弊风险因素。这些列举性风险因素是基于本款讨论的存在舞弊时常见的三种状况分类的。

Note: The factors listed in AU sec. 316. 85 cover a broad range of situations and are only examples. Accordingly, the auditor might identify additional or different fraud risk factors.

注：过渡性审计准则第316. 85条列举的因素涵盖了宽泛的情形，而且，仅是举例。因此，审计师可能识别更多或不同的舞弊风险因素。

66. All three conditions discussed in the preceding paragraph are not required to be observed or evident to conclude that a fraud risk exists. The auditor might conclude that a fraud risk exists even when only one of these three conditions is present.

66. 所有前款讨论的三种情形不需要同时发现或证实，才能认为存在舞弊。审计师可以在仅仅出现三者之一时就可以认为存在舞弊风险。

67. Consideration of the Risk of Omitted, Incomplete, or Inaccurate Disclosures. The auditor's evaluation of fraud risk factors in accordance with paragraph 65 should include evaluation of how fraud could be perpetrated or concealed by presenting incomplete or inaccurate disclosures or by omitting ? disclosures that are necessary for the financial

67. 对于遗漏、不完整或不准确披露的风险的考虑。审计师遵照第65款舞弊风险因素的评价应当包括舞弊如何被以不完整或不准确的披露或者遗漏披露的方式所实施或掩盖，而这些披露是按照适

statements to be presented fairly in conformity with the applicable financial reporting framework.

当的财务报告框架公允披露财务报表所必需的。

68. Presumption of Fraud Risk Involving Improper Revenue Recognition. The auditor should presume that there is a fraud risk involving improper revenue recognition and evaluate which types of revenue, revenue transactions, or assertions may give rise to such risks.

68. 涉及不正确的收入确认舞弊风险的假设。审计师应当假设存在涉及不正确的收入确认舞弊风险，并评价可能引发这些风险的收入类型、收入交易或认定。

69. Consideration of the Risk of Management Override of Controls. The auditor's identification of fraud risks should include the risk of management override of controls.

69. 对于管理层越权风险的考虑。审计师的舞弊风险识别应当包括管理层凌驾于控制之上的风险。

Note: Controls over management override are important to effective internal control over financial reporting for all companies, and may be particularly important at smaller companies because of the increased involvement of senior management in performing controls and in the period - end financial reporting process. For smaller companies, the controls that address the risk of management override might be different from those at a larger company. For example, a smaller company might rely on more detailed oversight by the audit committee that focuses on the risk of manage-

注：针对管理层越权的控制对于公司财务报告内部控制的有效性是重要的，而且尤其是在较小的公司，因为高级管理层更多地参与实施控制和期末财务报告过程。对于较小的公司，处理管理层越权风险的控制可能不同于那些较大的公司。例如，较小的公司可能更多地依赖于审计委员会专注于管理层越权风险的监督。

ment override.

Factors Relevant to Identifying Significant Risks

与识别重大风险有关的因素

70. To determine whether an identified and assessed risk is a significant risk, the auditor should evaluate whether the risk requires special audit consideration because of the nature of the risk or the likelihood and potential magnitude of misstatement related to the risk.

70. 为了确定已识别和评定的风险是否为重大风险，审计师应当根据该风险的性质以及与该风险有关的错报的可能性和潜在严重性，评价该风险是否需要特别的审计考虑。

Note: The determination of whether a risk of material misstatement is a significant risk is based on inherent risk, without regard to the effect of controls.

注：确定某个重大错报风险是否为重大风险，是基于固有风险，而不论控制的影响。

71. Factors that should be evaluated in determining which risks are significant risks include:

71. 在确定风险是否为重大风险时，应当评价的因素包括：

a. The effect of the quantitative and qualitative risk factors discussed in paragraph 60 on the likelihood and potential magnitude of misstatements;

a. 第 60 款讨论的数量和质量风险因素对于错报的可能性和潜在严重性的影响；

b. Whether the risk is a fraud risk;

b. 该风险是否为舞弊风险；

Note: A fraud risk is a significant risk.

注：舞弊风险是重大风险。

c. Whether the risk is related to recent significant economic, accounting, or other developments;

c. 该风险是否与近期重大经济、会计或其他发展有关；

d. The complexity of transactions;

d. 交易的复杂性；

e. Whether the risk involves significant transactions with related parties;

e. 该风险是否涉及与关联方的重大交易；

f. The degree of complexity or judgment in the recognition or measurement of financial information related to the risk, especially those measurements involving a wide range of measurement uncertainty; and

f. 在与风险有关的财务信息的确认或核算中所做判断的复杂程度，特别是涉及较宽泛的计量不确定性的那些核算；和

g. Whether the risk involves significant transactions that are outside the normal course of business for the company or that otherwise appear to be unusual due to their timing, size, or nature.

g. 该风险是否涉及该公司日常经营活动之外的重大交易，或者因其时间、大小和性质显得不同寻常。

Further Consideration of Controls
控制的进一步考虑

72. When the auditor has determined that a significant risk, including a fraud risk, exists, the auditor should evaluate the design of

72. 当审计师已经确定存在某个重大风险，包括舞弊风险，如果审计师尚未

the company's controls that are intended to address fraud risks and other significant risks and determine whether those controls have been implemented, if the auditor has not already done so when obtaining an understanding of internal control, as described in paragraphs 18 – 40 of this standard. [36]

按照本准则第 18 至 40 款的要求了解内部控制，那么审计师应当评价那些用于处理舞弊风险的公司控制的设计，并确定其是否已被执行。

73. Controls that address fraud risks include (a) specific controls designed to mitigate specific risks of fraud, e. g. , controls to address risks of intentional misstatement of specific accounts and (b) controls designed to prevent, deter, and detect fraud, e. g. , controls to promote a culture of honesty and ethical behavior. [37] Such controls also include those that address the risk of management override of other controls.

73. 处理舞弊风险的控制包括（a）特别设计用来降低舞弊风险的控制，比如，处理特定账户的故意错报风险的控制，和（b）设计用来防范、推迟和发现舞弊的控制，比如，提倡诚信和道德行为的文化的控制。这些控制还包括处理管理层越权的控制。

Revision of Risk Assessment
风险评估的修订

74. The auditor's assessment of the risks of material misstatement, including fraud risks, should continue throughout the audit. When the auditor obtains audit evidence during the course of the audit that contradicts the audit evidence on which the auditor originally

74. 审计师的重大错报风险评估，包括舞弊风险的评估，应当贯穿整个审计。当审计师在审计过程中取得的审计证据否定了最初的风险评估所依据的

based his or her risk assessment, the auditor should revise the risk assessment and modify planned audit procedures or perform additional procedures in response to the revised risk assessments. ㊳

证据，审计师应当修正风险评估，修改预定审计程序，或为修订后的风险评估而实施补充程序。

---

① Paragraphs 5 - 8 of Auditing Standard No. 8, Audit Risk.

审计准则第 8 号［审计风险］第 5 至 8 款。

② Terms defined in Appendix A, Definitions, are set in **boldface type** the first time they appear.

附录 A［定义］中的条目在正文中首次出现时采用**粗体字**。

③ AU sec. 316, Consideration of Fraud in a Financial Statement Audit, discusses fraud, its characteristics, and the types of misstatements due to fraud that are relevant to the audit, i. e. , misstatements arising from fraudulent financial reporting and misstatements arising from asset misappropriation.

过渡性审计准则第 316 条［财务报表审计中对于舞弊的考虑］讨论舞弊及其特点，与审计相关的由舞弊造成的错报的类型，例如，欺骗性财务报告引起的错报和挪用资产引起的错报。

④ Auditing Standard No. 15, Audit Evidence, describes further audit procedures as consisting of tests of controls and substantive procedures.

审计准则第 15 号［审计证据］规定了控制测试和实质性程序的进一步审计程序。

⑤ Paragraph 11 of Auditing Standard No. 15 discusses financial statement assertions.

审计准则第 15 号第 11 款讨论了财务报表认定。

⑥ The auditor should look to the requirements of the Securities and Exchange Commission for the company under audit with respect to the accounting principles applicable to that company.

审计师应当留意美国证券交易委员会关于该被审计公司所适用的会计政策的有关要求。

⑦ AU sec. 317, Illegal Acts by Clients, discusses the auditor's consideration of laws and regulations relevant to the audit.

过渡性审计准则第 317 条［客户的违法行为］讨论了审计对于与审计相关的法律和法规的考虑。

⑧ Paragraphs 21 - 22 of this standard discuss components of internal control over financial reporting.

本准则第 21 至 22 款讨论了财务报告内部控制的组成部分。

⑨ Paragraph 13 of Auditing Standard No. 5, An Audit of Internal Control Over Financial Reporting That is Integrated with An Audit of Financial Statements, states, "The size and complexity of the company, its business processes, and business units, may affect the way in which the company achieves many of its control objectives. The size and complexity of the company also might affect the risks of misstatement and the controls necessary to address those risks."

审计准则第 5 号［与财务报表审计合并执行的财务报告内部控制审计］第 13 款指出“公司的大小和复杂性、经营过程和业务单元会影响公司达成其众多控制目标的方式。公司的大小和复杂性也会影响错报风险以及处理这些风险所需的控制。”

⑩ Paragraph 10 of Auditing Standard No. 15.

审计准则第 15 号第 10 款。

⑪ Different internal control frameworks use different terms and approaches to describe the components of internal control over financial reporting.

不同的内部控制框架采用不同的术语和方法表述财务报告内部控制的组成部分。

⑫ See Securities Exchange Act Release No. 34 –47986 (June 5, 2003) for a description of the characteristics of a suitable, recognized framework.

关于适宜、被认可框架的特点的表述参见美国证券交易法第 34 –47987 号公告（2003 年 6 月 5 日）。

⑬ Paragraph 5 of Auditing Standard No. 5.

审计准则第 5 号第 5 款。

⑭ Paragraph 25 of Auditing Standard No. 5.

审计准则第 5 号第 25 款。

⑮ Paragraph A3 of Auditing Standard No. 5.

审计准则第 5 号第 A3 款。

⑯ Examples of such events and conditions include depreciation and amortization and conditions affecting the recoverability of assets.

这些事件和状况包括影响资产重置能力的折旧、摊销和状态。

⑰ Paragraphs 12 –13 of this standard.

本准则第 12 至 13 款。

⑱ Also see paragraph B5 of Appendix B of this standard.

参见本准则附录 B 第 B5 款。

⑲ In some companies, internal auditors or others performing an equivalent function contribute to the monitoring of controls. AU sec. 322, The auditor's Consideration of the Internal Audit Function in an Audit of Financial Statements, establishes requirements regarding the auditor's consideration and use of the work of the internal audit function.

在某些公司，内部审计师或其他履行同样职责的人员参与了控制的监督。过渡性审计准则第

322 条［审计师在财务报告内部控制审计中对于内部审计职能的考虑］为审计师考虑和利用内部审计部门的工作制定要求。

⑳ See paragraphs 34 – 38 of Auditing Standard No. 5.

参见审计准则第 5 号第 34 至 38 款。

㉑ Paragraphs 16 – 35 of Auditing Standard No. 13, The auditor's Responses to the Risks of Material Misstatement.

审计准则第 13 号［审计师对于重大错报风险的应对策略］第 16 至 35 款。

㉒ Paragraph B1 of Auditing Standard No. 5.

审计准则第 5 号第 B1 款。

㉓ Paragraph 22 of Auditing Standard No. 5.

审计准则第 5 号第 22 款。

㉔ The entity – level controls included in paragraph 24 of Auditing Standard No. 5 include controls related to the control environment; the company's risk assessment process; centralized processing and controls; controls over the period – end financial reporting process; and controls to monitor other controls.

审计准则第 5 号第 24 款的实体层面控制包括与公司控制环境相关的控制、公司的风险评估过程、集中化处理和控制、期末财务报告过程控制以及监督其他控制的控制。

㉕ See PCAOB Rule 3501 (a) (i), which defines "affiliate of the accounting firm."

参见 PCAOB 规则第 3501（a）（i）关于"事务所的成员所"的定义。

㉖ Paragraph 7 of Auditing Standard No. 9, Audit Planning.

审计准则第 9 号［审计计划］第 7 款。

㉗ Analytical procedures consist of evaluations of financial information made by a study of plausible relationships among both financial and nonfinancial data.

分析性程序由财务信息的评价构成，它是对财务和非财务数据貌似合理的关联关系的研究。

㉘ Paragraphs 52 – 53 of this standard.

本准则第 52 至 53 款。

㉙ See also paragraph 29 of Auditing Standard No. 14, Evaluating Audit Results.

参见审计准则第 14 号［评价审计结果］第 29 款。

㉚ AU sec. 316. 13.

过渡性审计准则第 316. 13 条。

㉛ Paragraphs 20 – 23 of Auditing Standard No. 14 establish further requirements for evaluating whether misstatements might be indicative of fraud and determining the necessary procedures to be performed in those situations.

审计准则第14号第22至23款为评价错报是否暗示存在舞弊和确定在这些情况下所需实施的程序制定进一步的要求。

㉜ Paragraphs 16 – 35 of Auditing Standard No. 13.

审计准则第13号第16至35款。

㉝ Paragraph A10 of Auditing Standard No. 5 states:

审计准则第5号第A10款指出:

An account or disclosure is a significant account or disclosure if there is a reasonable possibility that the account or disclosure could contain a misstatement that, individually or when aggregated with others, has a material effect on the financial statements, considering the risks of both overstatement and understatement. The determination of whether an account or disclosure is significant is based on inherent risk, without regard to the effect of controls.

如果某个账户或披露合理的可能存在错报，而该错报单独或与其他错报合并，对于财务报表存在重大影响，同时考虑高报和低报两种风险，那么，该账户或披露就是重要账户或披露。确定账户或披露是否重要是基于固有风险，而不论控制的影响。

㉞ Paragraph A9 of Auditing Standard No. 5 states:

审计准则第5号第A9款指出:

A relevant assertion is a financial statement assertion that has a reasonable possibility of containing a misstatement or misstatements that would cause the financial statements to be materially misstated. The determination of whether an assertion is a relevant assertion is based on inherent risk, without regard to the effect of controls.

相关认定是合理的可能存在导致财务报表重大错报的错报的财务认定。确定某个认定是否是相关认定是基于固有风险，而不论控制的影响。

㉟ The auditor might perform substantive auditing procedures because his or her assessment of the risk that undetected misstatement would cause the financial statements to be materially misstated is unacceptably high or as a means of introducing unpredictability in the procedures performed. See paragraphs 11, 14, and 25 of Auditing Standard No. 14, for further discussion about undetected misstatement. See paragraph 61 of Auditing Standard No. 5 and paragraph 5. c. of Auditing Standard No. 13, for further discussion about the unpredictability of auditing procedures.

如果审计师对于可能导致财务报表重大错报的未发现错报的风险评估高得不可接受，或者，作为在实施的程序中引入不可预见性的方法（避免审计对象预先知道审计师的程序，译者注），那么，审计师可以实施实质性审计程序。

㊱ Auditing Standard No. 13 discusses the auditor's response to fraud risks and other significant risks.

审计准则第 13 号讨论了审计师对于舞弊和其他重大风险的应对策略。

㊲ AU sec. 316. 88 and paragraph 14 of Auditing Standard No. 5 present examples of controls that address fraud risks.

过渡性审计准则第 316. 88 条和审计准则第 5 号第 14 款列举了处理舞弊风险的控制。

㊳ See also paragraph 46 of Auditing Standard No. 13.

参见审计准则第 13 号第 46 款。

Appendix A - Definitions

附录 A - 定义

A1. For purposes of this standard, the terms listed below are defined as follows:

A1. 就本准则而言，下列用语的定义是：

A2. Business risks - Risks that result from significant conditions, events, circumstances, actions, or inactions that could adversely affect a company's ability to achieve its objectives and execute its strategies. Business risks also might result from setting inappropriate objectives and strategies or from changes or complexity in the company's operations or management.

A2. 经营风险：由于重大状况、事件、情况、作为或不作为而对于公司达成其目标和实施其战略的能力造成负面影响的风险。经营风险可能源自设定不适当的目标和战略，或者公司运营或管理的变革和复杂性。

A3. Company's objectives and strategies - The overall plans for the company as established by management or the board of directors. Strategies are the approaches by which management intends to achieve its objectives.

A3. 公司目标和战略：公司管理层或者董事会制定的公司总体计划。战略是管理层意图采取的达成其目标的方法。

A4. Risk assessment procedures – The procedures performed by the auditor to obtain information for identifying and assessing the risks of material misstatement in the financial statements whether due to error or fraud.

A4. 风险评估程序：审计师实施的用来获取识别和评估由于错误或舞弊造成的财务报表重大错报风险的程序。

Note: Risk assessment procedures by themselves do not provide sufficient appropriate evidence on which to base an audit opinion.

注：风险评估程序本身不能为审计意见提供充分适当的证据。

A5. Significant risk – A risk of material misstatement that requires special audit consideration.

A5. 重大风险：需要特别审计关注的重大错报风险。

Appendix B – Consideration of Manual and Automated Systems and Controls

附录B – 对人工和自动系统及控制的考虑

B1. While obtaining an understanding of the company's information system related to financial reporting, the auditor should obtain an understanding of how the company uses information technology ("IT") and how IT affects the financial statements. [①] The auditor also should obtain an understanding of the extent of manual controls and automated controls used by the company, including the IT general controls that are important to the effective operation of the automated con-

B1. 在了解与财务报告相关的公司信息系统时，审计师应当了解该公司如何运用信息系统（“IT”）以及 IT 如何影响财务报表。审计师还应当了解该公司运用人工和自动控制的范围，包括对于自动控制有效运行而言重要的 IT 一般控制。该资料应当在评估重大错报风险时考虑

trols. That information should be taken into account in assessing the risks of material misstatement. ②

在内。

B2. Controls in a manual system might include procedures such as approvals and reviews of transactions, and reconciliations and follow – up of reconciling items.

B2. 人工系统的控制可能包括交易的审批和复核、调节和调节事项的跟进等程序。

B3. Alternatively, a company might use automated procedures to initiate, record, process, and report transactions, in which case records in electronic format would replace paper documents. When IT is used to initiate, record, process, and report transactions, the IT systems and programs may include controls related to the relevant assertions of significant accounts and disclosures or may be critical to the effective functioning of manual controls that depend on IT.

B3. 换言之，公司可以利用自动程序发起、登记、处理和报告其交易，此时，电子记录会代替书面文件。当利用 IT 发起、登记、处理和报告交易时，IT 系统和程序可能包括与重要账户和披露相关认定有关的控制，或者，对于依赖 IT 的人工控制的有效运行而言是关键的。

B4. The auditor should obtain an understanding of specific risks to a company's internal control over financial reporting resulting from IT. Examples of such risks include:

B4. 审计师应当了解 IT 导致的公司财务报告内部控制的具体风险。例如：

• Reliance on systems or programs that are inaccurately processing data, processing inaccurate data, or both;

• 依赖于不准确地处理数据、处理不准确的数据或者二者兼而有之的系统或程序；

• Unauthorized access to data that might result in destruction of data or improper changes to data, including the recording of unauthorized or non – existent transactions or inaccurate recording of transactions (particular risks might arise when multiple users access a common database);

• 未经授权访问数据，导致数据损坏或不适当地修改，包括记录未经授权的或不存在的交易，或者交易的不准确记录（具体的风险可能源自多用户访问共享数据库）；

• The possibility of IT personnel gaining access privileges beyond those necessary to perform their assigned duties, thereby breaking down segregation of duties;

• IT 员工取得超过执行其职责所必需的访问权限，从而打破了职责分工；

• Unauthorized changes to data in master files;

• 未经授权改变主文档；

• Unauthorized changes to systems or programs;

• 未经授权改变系统或程序；

• Failure to make necessary changes to systems or programs;

• 未能对系统和程序进行必要地修改；

• Inappropriate manual intervention; and

• 不适当的人工干预；和

• Potential loss of data or inability to access data as required.

• 潜在的数据丢失或不能按照要求访问数据。

B5. In obtaining an understanding of the company's control activities, the auditor should obtain an understanding of how the company

B5. 在了解公司的控制活动时，审计师应当了解该公司如何应对 IT 引发的

has responded to risks arising from IT.

风险。

B6. When a company uses manual elements in internal control systems and the auditor plans to rely on, and therefore test, those manual controls, the auditor should design procedures to test the consistency in the application of those manual controls.

B6. 当公司在控制系统中利用人工，且审计师计划依赖并测试这些人工控制时，审计师应当设计程序，测试这些人工控制的一致性。

① See also AU sec. 324, Service Organizations, if the company uses a service organization for services that are part of the company's internal control over financial reporting.

如果公司利用服务组织的服务作为公司财务报告内部控制的一部分，参见过渡性审计准则第324条［服务组织］。

② See also paragraphs 16 – 17 of Auditing Standard No. 9, Audit Planning.

参见审计准则第9号［审计计划］第16至17款。

December 15, 2010

2010 年 12 月 15 日

AUDITING AND RELATED PROFESSIONAL PRACTICE STANDARDS

审计及相关专业实务准则

Auditing Standard No. 13 –

审计准则第 13 号 —

The auditor's Responses to the Risks of Material Misstatement

审计师对于重大错报风险的应对策略

PCAOB

Public Company Accounting Oversight Board

公众公司会计监管委员会

[Effective pursuant to SEC Release No. 34 – 63606, File No. PCAOB – 2010 – 01, December 23, 2010]

[按照 SEC 第 34 – 63606 号公告生效；文件号：PCAOB – 2010 – 01，2012 年 12 月 23 日]

Final Rule: PCAOB Release No. 2010 – 004

最终规则：PCAOB 公告第 2010 – 004 号

Table of Contents

目　　录

Paragraph

款　　号

Introduction
引　　言

1. This standard establishes requirements regarding designing and implementing appropriate responses to the risks of material misstatement.

1. 本准则为设计和执行重大错报风险的适当应对策略制定要求。

Objective
目　　标

2. The objective of the auditor is to address the risks of material misstatement through appropriate overall audit responses and audit procedures.

2. 审计师的目标是通过适当的总体审计应对策略和审计程序处理重大错报风险。

Responding to the Risks of Material Misstatement
应对重大错报风险

3. To meet the objective in the preceding paragraph, the auditor must design and implement audit responses that address the risks of material misstatement that are identified and assessed in accordance with Auditing Standard No. 12, Identifying and Assessing Risks of Material Misstatement.

3. 为了满足前款的目标，审计师必须设计和执行审计应对策略，处理遵循审计准则第 12 号［识别和评估重大错报风险］所识别和评估的重大错报风险。

4. This standard discusses the following types of audit responses:

4. 本准则讨论以下类型的审计应对策略：

a. Responses that have an overall effect on how the audit is conducted ("overall responses"), as described in paragraphs 5 – 7; and

a. 如第5至7款所述的对于审计如何实施有总体影响的应对策略（“总体应对策略”）；和

b. Responses involving the nature, timing, and extent of the audit procedures to be performed, as described in paragraphs 8 – 46.

b. 如第8至46款所述的涉及将要实施的审计程序性质、时间和范围的应对策略。

Overall Responses
总体应对策略

5. The auditor should design and implement overall responses to address the assessed risks of material misstatement as follows:

5. 审计师应当设计和执行总体应对策略，以如下方式处理评定的重大错报风险：

a. Making appropriate assignments of significant engagement responsibilities. The knowledge, skill, and ability of engagement team members with significant engagement responsibilities should be commensurate with the assessed risks of material misstatement. ①

a. 适当分配重大业务责任。承担重大业务责任的业务团队成员的知识、技术和能力应当与评定的重大错报风险相一致。

b. Providing the extent of supervision that is appropriate for the circumstances, including, in particular, the assessed risks of material misstatement. (See paragraphs 5 – 6 of Auditing Standard No. 10, Supervision of the Audit Engagement.)

b. 提供的监督范围要与具体情况相适应，尤其是评定的重大错报风险。（参见审计准则第10号［审计业务的监督］第5–6款）

c. Incorporating elements of unpredictability in the selection of audit procedures to be performed. As part of the auditor's response to the assessed risks of material misstatement, including the assessed risks of material misstatement due to fraud ("fraud risks"), the auditor should incorporate an element of unpredictability in the selection of auditing procedures to be performed from year to year. Examples of ways to incorporate an element of unpredictability include:

c. 在选择将要实施的审计程序时加入不可预见因素。作为审计师对于评定的重大错报风险应对策略的一部分，包括评定的舞弊导致的重大错报风险（“舞弊风险”），审计师应当逐年在选择将要实施的审计程序时加入不可预见因素。加入不可预见因素的方法包括：

(1) Performing audit procedures related to accounts, disclosures, and assertions that would not otherwise be tested based on their amount or the auditor's assessment of risk;

（1）对以其金额或审计师风险评估而言不会被测试的账户、披露和认定实施审计程序；

(2) Varying the timing of the audit procedures;

（2）变更审计程序的时间；

(3) Selecting items for testing that have lower amounts or are otherwise outside customary selection parameters;

（3）选择那些较小金额的项目或在常见选择参数之外的项目测试；

(4) Performing audit procedures on an unannounced basis; and

（4）不经宣布就实施审计程序；和

(5) In multi-location audits, varying the location or the nature, timing, and extent of audit procedures at related locations or busi-

（5）在多场所审计中，每年改变在相关场所或业务单元的审计程序的场所

ness units from year to year. [2]

或性质、时间和范围。

d. Evaluating the company's selection and application of significant accounting principles. The auditor should evaluate whether the company's selection and application of significant accounting principles, particularly those related to subjective measurements and complex transactions, [3] are indicative of bias that could lead to material misstatement of the financial statements.

d. 评价公司对于重大会计政策的选择和运用。审计师应当评价公司对于重大会计政策的选择和运用，尤其是与主观指标和复杂交易有关的那些会计政策，是否暗示存在导致财务报表重大错报的偏好。

6. The auditor also should determine whether it is necessary to make pervasive changes to the nature, timing, or extent of audit procedures to adequately address the assessed risks of material misstatement. Examples of such pervasive changes include modifying the audit strategy to:

6. 审计师还应当确定是否需要广泛地改变审计程序的性质、时间或范围，以便充分地处理评定的重大错报风险。这些广泛改变包括修改审计策略从而：

a. Increase the substantive testing of the valuation of numerous significant accounts at year end because of significantly deteriorating market conditions, and

a. 针对显著恶化的市场状况，在年末对大量重要账户的评估增加实质性程序，和

b. Obtain more persuasive audit evidence from substantive procedures due to the identification of pervasive weaknesses in the company's control environment.

b. 由于识别到公司控制环境的广泛缺陷，从实质性程序获取更具说服力的审计证据。

7. Due professional care requires the auditor to exercise professional skepticism. ④ Professional skepticism is an attitude that includes a questioning mind and a critical assessment of the appropriateness and sufficiency of audit evidence. The auditor's responses to the assessed risks of material misstatement, particularly fraud risks, should involve the application of professional skepticism in gathering and evaluating audit evidence. ⑤ Examples of the application of professional skepticism in response to the assessed fraud risks are (a) modifying the planned audit procedures to obtain more reliable evidence regarding relevant assertions and (b) obtaining sufficient appropriate evidence to corroborate management's explanations or representations concerning important matters, such as through third – party confirmation, use of a specialist engaged or employed by the auditor, or examination of documentation from independent sources.

7. 职业审慎要求审计师践行职业怀疑。职业怀疑是一种态度，包括质疑的心态和对审计证据的适当性和充分性的评判性评估。审计师对于评定的重大错报风险的处理，尤其是舞弊风险，应当包括在收集和评价审计证据时运用职业审慎。在处理舞弊风险时运用职业审慎包括（a）修改预定审计程序获取更多可靠的相关认定的证据，和（b）获取充分适当的有关重大事项的证据印证管理层的解释或声明，比如，通过第三方函证，利用审计师聘用或雇用的专家，或者，检查来自独立来源的文档。

Responses Involving the Nature , Timing , and Extent of Audit Procedures

涉及审计程序性质、时间和范围的应对策略

8. The auditor should design and perform audit procedures in a manner that addresses the

8. 审计师应当为每个重要账户和披露的每个相关

assessed risks of material misstatement for each relevant assertion of each significant account and disclosure.

认定的重大错报风险而设计和实施审计程序。

9. In designing the audit procedures to be performed, the auditor should:

9. 在设计将要实施的审计程序时，审计师应当：

a. Obtain more persuasive audit evidence the higher the auditor's assessment of risk;

a. 更高的风险评估需要获取更有说服力的审计证据；

b. Take into account the types of potential misstatements that could result from the identified risks and the likelihood and magnitude of potential misstatement; ⑥

b. 将已识别风险可能造成的潜在错报的类型以及潜在错报的可能性和严重性考虑在内；

c. In an integrated audit, design the testing of controls to accomplish the objectives of both audits simultaneously:

c. 在整合审计中，为同时达成两种审计目标设计控制测试：

(1) To obtain sufficient evidence to support the auditor's control risk⑦ assessments for purposes of the audit of financial statements; ⑧ and

(1) 获取充分的证据支持审计师为财务报表审计所做的控制风险评估；和

(2) To obtain sufficient evidence to support the auditor's opinion on internal control over financial reporting as of year – end.

(2) 获取充分的证据支持审计师发表截至年末的财务报告内部控制审计意见。

Note: Auditing Standard No. 5 establishes requirements for tests of controls in the audit

注：审计准则第 5 号为财务报告内部控制审计的控

of internal control over financial reporting.

制测试制定要求。

10. The audit procedures performed in response to the assessed risks of material misstatement can be classified into two categories: (1) tests of controls and (2) substantive procedures. ⑨ Paragraphs 16 – 35 of this standard discuss tests of controls, and paragraphs 36 – 46 discuss substantive procedures.

10. 为了应对评定的重大错报风险实施的审计程序可以被分为两类：（1）控制测试和（2）实质性程序。本准则第 16 至 35 款讨论控制测试，第 36 至 46 款讨论实质性程序。

Note: Paragraphs 16 – 17 of this standard discuss when tests of controls are necessary in a financial statement audit. Ordinarily, tests of controls are performed for relevant assertions for which the auditor chooses to rely on controls to modify his or her substantive procedures.

注：本准则第 16 至 17 款讨论财务报表审计何时需要控制测试。通常，对于审计师选择依赖于控制而改变其实质性程序时，需要对相关认定实施控制测试。

Responses to Significant Risks

重大风险的应对策略

11. For significant risks, the auditor should perform substantive procedures, including tests of details, that are specifically responsive to the assessed risks.

11. 对于重大风险，审计师应当实施具体应对评定风险的实质性程序，包括详细测试。

Note: Auditing Standard No. 12 discusses identification of significant risks ⑩ and states that fraud risks are significant risks.

注：审计准则第 12 号讨论重大风险的识别，并指出舞弊风险是重大风险。

Responses to Fraud Risks
舞弊风险的应对策略

12. The audit procedures that are necessary to address the assessed fraud risks depend upon the types of risks and the relevant assertions that might be affected.

12. 处理评定的舞弊风险所需的审计程序依赖于风险的种类和可能受到影响的相关认定。

Note: If the auditor identifies deficiencies in controls that are intended to address assessed fraud risks, the auditor should take into account those deficiencies when designing his or her response to those fraud risks.

注:如果审计师识别的控制缺陷是用于处理评定的舞弊风险,审计师应当在设计这些舞弊风险的应对策略时将这些缺陷考虑在内。

Note: Auditing Standard No. 5 establishes requirements for addressing assessed fraud risks in the audit of internal control over financial reporting. [11]

注：审计准则第 5 号为财务报告内部控制审计中应对评定的舞弊风险制定要求。

13. Addressing Fraud Risks in the Audit of Financial Statements. In the audit of financial statements, the auditor should perform substantive procedures, including tests of details, that are specifically responsive to the assessed fraud risks. If the auditor selects certain controls intended to address the assessed fraud risks for testing in accordance with paragraphs 16 – 17 of this standard, the auditor should perform tests of those controls.

13. 在财务报表审计中处理舞弊风险。在财务报表审计中，审计师应当实施具体应对评定舞弊风险的实质性程序，包括详细测试。如果审计师遵照本准则第 16 至 17 款选择测试用来处理评定舞弊风险的特定控制，审计师应当实施这些控制的测试。

14. The following are examples of ways in which planned audit procedures may be modified to address assessed fraud risks:

14. 以下是为了处理评定舞弊风险而可能修改预定审计程序的方法举例：

a. Changing the nature of audit procedures to obtain evidence that is more reliable or to obtain additional corroborative information;

a. 改变审计程序的性质，获取更可靠的证据，或者获取进一步的印证资料；

b. Changing the timing of audit procedures to be closer to the end of the period or to the points during the period in which fraudulent transactions are more likely to occur; and

b. 将审计程序的时间改为更加靠近期末或舞弊交易更可能发生的那些时点；和

c. Changing the extent of the procedures applied to obtain more evidence, e. g., by increasing sample sizes or applying computer-assisted audit techniques to all of the items in an account.

c. 改变审计程序的范围，获取更多证据，比如，增加样本数量或者对于某个账户的全部项目使用计算机辅助审计技术。

Note: AU secs. 316. 54 – . 67 provide additional examples of responses to assessed fraud risks relating to fraudulent financial reporting (e. g., revenue recognition, inventory quantities, and management estimates) and misappropriation of assets in the audit of financial statements.

注：过渡审计准则第 316.54 至 .67 条提供了更多的在财务报表审计中应对与舞弊性财务报告和挪用资产有关的评定舞弊风险的举例(比如,收入确认、存货数量和管理层估计)。

15. Also, AU sec. 316 indicates that the auditor should perform audit procedures to specifically address the risk of management o-

15. 另外，过渡审计准则第 316 条指出审计师应当实施审计程序专门处理管

verride of controls including:

理层凌驾于控制之上的风险，包括：

a. Examining journal entries and other adjustments for evidence of possible material misstatement due to fraud (AU secs. 316.58 – .62);

a. 检查会计分录和其他调整，寻找舞弊导致的可能的重大错报的证据（过渡审计准则第 316.58 至 .62 条）；

b. Reviewing accounting estimates for biases that could result in material misstatement due to fraud (AU secs. 316.63 – .65); and

b. 审查会计估计，寻找舞弊导致的可能造成重大错报的偏好（过渡审计准则第 316.63 至 .65 条）；和

c. Evaluating the business rationale for significant unusual transactions (AU secs. 316.66 – .67).

c. 评价重大非常规交易的商业根据（过渡审计准则第 316.66 至 .67 条）。

Testing Controls
控制测试

Testing Controls in an Audit of Financial Statements
财务报表审计的控制测试

16. Controls to be Tested. If the auditor plans to assess control risk at less than the maximum by relying on controls, [12] and the nature, timing, and extent of planned substantive procedures are based on that lower as-

16. 将被测试的控制。如果审计师打算将控制风险评为低于最大风险从而依赖于控制，并且，预定实质性程序的性质、时间和

sessment, the auditor must obtain evidence that the controls selected for testing are designed effectively and operated effectively during the entire period of reliance. [13] However, the auditor is not required to assess control risk at less than the maximum for all relevant assertions and, for a variety of reasons, the auditor may choose not to do so.

范围都基于该较低评估，审计师必须获取受测的选定控制在整个受信期间是有效设计和运行的证据。但是，审计师不必将所有相关认定评估为低于最大水平，审计师有很多理由不选择这样做。

17. Also, tests of controls must be performed in the audit of financial statements for each relevant assertion for which substantive procedures alone cannot provide sufficient appropriate audit evidence and when necessary to support the auditor's reliance on the accuracy and completeness of financial information used in performing other audit procedures. [14]

17. 另外，在财务报表审计中，对于实质性程序不能单独提供充分适当的审计证据的每个相关认定，必须实施控制测试，并支持审计师用于实施其他审计程序所依赖的财务资料的准确性和完整性。

Note: When a significant amount of information supporting one or more relevant assertions is electronically initiated, recorded, processed, or reported, it might be impossible to design effective substantive tests that, by themselves, would provide sufficient appropriate evidence regarding the assertions. For such assertions, significant audit evidence may be available only in electronic form. In such ca-

注:当支持某个或多个相关认定的大量资料是以电子方式发起、登记、处理或报告时,几乎不可能仅仅依靠设计有效的实质性程序就为该认定提供充分适当的证据。对于这些认定,大量的审计证据只能来自电子形式。此时,审计证据的充

ses, the sufficiency and appropriateness of the audit evidence usually depend on the effectiveness of controls over their accuracy and completeness. Furthermore, the potential for improper initiation or alteration of information to occur and not be detected may be greater if information is initiated, recorded, processed, or reported only in electronic form and appropriate controls are not operating effectively.

分性和适当性取决于其准确性和完整性控制的有效性。进一步而言，如果信息仅以电子形式发起、登记、处理或报告，并且适当的控制没有有效运行，那么，发生不适当的发起或更改信息并且不被发现的潜在可能性会更大。

18. Evidence about the Effectiveness of Controls in the Audit of Financial Statements. In designing and performing tests of controls for the audit of financial statements, the evidence necessary to support the auditor's control risk assessment depends on the degree of reliance the auditor plans to place on the effectiveness of a control. The auditor should obtain more persuasive audit evidence from tests of controls the greater the reliance the auditor places on the effectiveness of a control. The auditor also should obtain more persuasive evidence about the effectiveness of controls for each relevant assertion for which the audit approach consists primarily of tests of controls, including situations in which substantive procedures alone cannot provide sufficient appropriate audit evidence.

18. 财务报告内部控制有效性的证据。在设计和实施财务报告内部控制有效性测试时，支持审计师的控制风险评估所需的证据取决于审计师对于控制有效性所计划的依赖程度。审计师越依赖控制的有效性，就应该从控制测试中获取更有说服力的审计证据。对于主要由控制测试构成的审计方法，包括实质性程序不能单独提供充分适当的审计证据的情况，审计师还应当为每个相关认定的控制有效性获取更有说服力的证据。

Testing Design Effectiveness

测试设计有效性

19. The auditor should test the design effectiveness of the controls selected for testing by determining whether the company's controls, if they are operated as prescribed by persons possessing the necessary authority and competence to perform the control effectively, satisfy the company's control objectives and can effectively prevent or detect error or fraud that could result in material misstatements in the financial statements.

19. 审计师应当测试公司的控制有效性，是否由具备必要权力和胜任能力的人员按照规定有效地执行，从而满足公司的控制目标和有效地防范或发现可能导致财务报表重大错报的错误或舞弊。

Note: A smaller, less complex company might achieve its control objectives in a different manner from a larger, more complex organization. For example, a smaller, less complex company might have fewer employees in the accounting function, limiting opportunities to segregate duties and leading the company to implement alternative controls to achieve its control objectives. In such circumstances, the auditor should evaluate whether those alternative controls are effective.

注：较小的不太复杂的公司可以采取不同于较大的较复杂组织的方式达成其控制目标。例如，较小的不太复杂的公司可能有较少的会计部门员工，限制了职责分工的机会，并导致公司执行替代控制来达到其控制目标。在这些情况下，审计师应当评价这些替代控制是否有效。

20. Procedures the auditor performs to test design effectiveness include a mix of inquiry of appropriate personnel , observation of the

20. 审计师测试设计有效性的程序包括询问适当的员工、观察公司的运营和

company's operations, and inspection of relevant documentation. Walkthroughs that include these procedures ordinarily are sufficient to evaluate design effectiveness. ⑮

审查相关的文档等方式的组合。包含这些程序的穿行测试通常足以评价设计有效性。

Testing Operating Effectiveness
测试运行的有效性

21. The auditor should test the operating effectiveness of a control selected for testing by determining whether the control is operating as designed and whether the person performing the control possesses the necessary authority and competence to perform the control effectively.

21. 审计师应当通过确定控制是否按照设计运行，并且执行控制过程的人员是否具备必要的权力和胜任能力有效地执行控制，从而测试被选择测试的控制的运行有效性。

22. Procedures the auditor performs to test operating effectiveness include a mix of inquiry of appropriate personnel, observation of the company's operations, inspection of relevant documentation, and re-performance of the control.

22. 审计师测试运行有效性的程序包括询问适当的员工、观察公司的运营、审查相关的文档和重新执行控制等方式的组合。

Obtaining Evidence from Tests of Controls
从控制测试获取证据

23. The evidence provided by the auditor's tests of the effectiveness of controls depends upon the mix of the nature, timing, and extent of the auditor's procedures. Further, for

23. 审计师测试控制有效性提供的证据取决于审计程序的性质、时间和范围的组合。进一步而言，对

an individual control, different combinations of the nature, timing, and extent of testing might provide sufficient evidence in relation to the degree of reliance in an audit of financial statements.

于单个控制，测试的性质、时间和范围的不同组合可能为财务报表审计提供与信赖程度相关的充分证据。

Note: To obtain evidence about whether a control is effective, the control must be tested directly; the effectiveness of a control cannot be inferred from the absence of misstatements detected by substantive procedures.

注：为了获取控制有效性的证据，控制必须被直接测试；不能由于实质性程序没有发现错报而推测控制的有效性。

Nature of Tests of Controls
控制测试的性质

24. Some types of tests, by their nature, produce greater evidence of the effectiveness of controls than other tests. The following tests that the auditor might perform are presented in the order of the evidence that they ordinarily would produce, from least to most: inquiry, observation, inspection of relevant documentation, and re – performance of a control.

24. 某些控制类型因其性质而提供比其他测试更强的控制有效性的证据。下面按照所提供证据从弱到强的一般顺序列举了审计师可能实施的测试：询问、观察、审查相关文档和重新执行控制。

Note: Inquiry alone does not provide sufficient evidence to support a conclusion about the effectiveness of a control.

注：询问不能单独提供充分的证据支持控制有效性的结论。

25. The nature of the tests of controls that will provide appropriate evidence depends, to a large degree, on the nature of the control to be tested, including whether the operation of the control results in documentary evidence of its operation. Documentary evidence of the operation of some controls, such as management′s philosophy and operating style, might not exist.

25. 提供适当证据的 控制测试的性质很大程度上取决于受测控制的性质，包括控制的运行是否产生其运行的书面证据。某些控制运行的书面证据可能不存在，比如，管理层理念和经营风格。

Note: A smaller, less complex company or unit might have less formal documentation regarding the operation of its controls. In those situations, testing controls through inquiry combined with other procedures, such as observation of activities, inspection of less formal documentation, or re-performance of certain controls, might provide sufficient evidence about whether the control is effective.

注：较小的不太复杂的公司或业务单元可能只有不太正式的控制运行文档。在这些情况下，通过询问并结合其他程序，包括观察运营活动、审查不太正式的文档或者重新执行某些控制，所做的控制测试也许能提供控制是否有效的充分证据。

Extent of Tests of Controls
控制测试的范围

26. The more extensively a control is tested, the greater the evidence obtained from that test.

26. 控制测试越全面，测试所获证据越多。

27. Matters that could affect the necessary extent of testing of a control in relation to the

27. 可能影响与对控制的依赖程度有关的控制测试

degree of reliance on a control include the following:

的必要范围的事项包括：

- The frequency of the performance of the control by the company during the audit period;

- 该控制在审计期间执行的频率；

- The length of time during the audit period that the auditor is relying on the operating effectiveness of the control;

- 在审计期间审计师依赖该控制运行有效性的时间长度；

- The expected rate of deviation from a control;

- 某控制的预期差错率；

- The relevance and reliability of the audit evidence to be obtained regarding the operating effectiveness of the control;

- 将要获取的审计证据就该控制运行有效性而言的相关性和可靠性；

- The extent to which audit evidence is obtained from tests of other controls related to the assertion;

- 与该认定有关的其他控制测试中获取的审计证据的范围；

- The nature of the control, including, in particular, whether it is a manual control or an automated control; and

- 控制的性质，尤其是它是人工控制还是自动控制；和

- For an automated control, the effectiveness of relevant information technology general controls.

- 对于自动控制，相关的信息技术一般控制的有效性。

Note: AU sec. 350, Audit Sampling, establishes requirements regarding the use of sampling in tests of controls.

注：过渡审计准则第 350 条［审计抽样］为使用控制测试抽样制定要求。

Timing of Tests of Controls

控制测试的时间

28. The timing of tests of controls relates to when the evidence about the operating effectiveness of the controls is obtained and the period of time to which it applies. Paragraph 16 of this standard indicates that the auditor must obtain evidence that the controls selected for testing are designed effectively and operated effectively during the entire period of reliance.

28. 控制测试的时间与何时获取关于控制有效性证据以及该控制适用的期间有关。本准则第 16 款指出审计师必须获取被选择测试的控制在整个信赖期间都有效设计和有效运行的证据。

29. Using Audit Evidence Obtained during an Interim Period. When the auditor obtains evidence about the operating effectiveness of controls as of or through an interim date, he or she should determine what additional evidence is necessary concerning the operation of the controls for the remaining period of reliance.

29. 利用中期获取的审计证据。当审计师获取截至或贯穿中期时点的控制运行有效性的证据时，应当确定在剩余信赖期间，哪些有关控制运行有效性的补充证据是所需的。

30. The additional evidence that is necessary to update the results of testing from an interim date through the remaining period of reliance depends on the following factors:

30. 为了针对中期时点至剩余信赖期而更新测试结果所需的进一步证据取决于下列因素：

• The possibility that there have been any significant changes in internal control over financial reporting subsequent to the interim date;

• 中期时点之后发生财务报告内部控制重大变化的可能性；

Note: If there have been significant changes to the control since the interim date, the auditor should obtain evidence about the effectiveness of the new or modified control;

注：如果自中期时点控制已经发生重大变化，审计师应当获取新控制或已变更控制的有效性的证据；

• The inherent risk associated with the related account (s) or assertion (s);

• 与相关账户或认定有关的固有风险；

• The specific control tested prior to year end, including the nature of the control and the risk that the control is no longer effective during the remaining period, and the results of the tests of the control;

• 年末测试的特定控制，包括控制的性质和剩余期间控制不再有效的风险，以及控制测试的结果；

• The planned degree of reliance on the control;

• 对于控制的预定信赖程度；

• The sufficiency of the evidence of effectiveness obtained at an interim date; and

• 在中期时点获取的有效性证据的充分性；和

• The length of the remaining period.

• 剩余期间的长度。

31. Using Audit Evidence Obtained in Past Audits. For audits of financial statements, the auditor should obtain evidence during the

31. 利用以往审计获得的审计证据。对于财务报表审计，审计师应当在当年

current year audit about the design and operating effectiveness of controls upon which the auditor relies. When controls on which the auditor plans to rely have been tested in past audits and the auditor plans to use evidence about the effectiveness of those controls that was obtained in prior years, the auditor should take into account the following factors to determine the evidence needed during the current year audit to support the auditor's control risk assessments:

审计中获取其依赖的控制设计和运行有效性的证据。当审计师计划依赖的控制已经在以往的审计中被测试过，而且审计师计划利用以往年度获取的这些控制的有效性证据，那么，审计师应当在确定本年度支持其控制风险评估所需的证据时，将下列因素考虑在内：

• The nature and materiality of misstatements that the control is intended to prevent or detect;

• 控制用于防范或发现错报的性质和重要性；

• The inherent risk associated with the related account (s) or assertion (s);

• 与相关账户或认定相关的固有风险；

• Whether there have been changes in the volume or nature of transactions that might adversely affect control design or operating effectiveness;

• 是否发生了可能对控制的设计或运行有效性造成不利影响的交易数量或性质方面的变化；

• Whether the account has a history of errors;

• 该账户是否有过错误；

• The effectiveness of entity - level controls that the auditor has tested, especially controls that monitor other controls;

• 审计师已经测试的实体层面控制的有效性，尤其是监督其他控制的控制；

- The nature of the controls and the frequency with which they operate;

- 控制的性质及其运行的频率；

- The degree to which the control relies on the effectiveness of other controls (e. g. , the control environment or information technology general controls);

- 该控制依赖于其他控制有效性的程度（比如，控制环境或信息技术一般控制）；

- The competence of the personnel who perform the control or monitor its performance and whether there have been changes in key personnel who perform the control or monitor its performance;

- 执行控制或监督其执行人员的胜任能力，以及执行控制或监督其执行的关键人员是否已改变；

- Whether the control relies on performance by an individual or is automated (i. e. , an automated control would generally be expected to be lower risk if relevant information technology general controls are effective); [16]

- 该控制是依赖于个人的执行，还是自动化的（比如，如果相关的信息技术一般控制是有效的，那么，自动化控制通常认为风险较低）；

- The complexity of the control and the significance of the judgments that must be made in connection with its operation;

- 控制的复杂性和做出与该操作有关的判断的重大性；

- The planned degree of reliance on the control;

- 对于该控制的预定信赖程度；

- The nature, timing, and extent of procedures performed in past audits;

- 以往审计执行程序的性质、时间和范围；

• The results of the previous years' testing of the control;

• 该控制以往年度的测试结果；

• Whether there have been changes in the control or the process in which it operates since the previous audit; and

• 自上次审计以来该控制或其处理是否已经发生变化；和

• For integrated audits, the evidence regarding the effectiveness of the controls obtained during the audit of internal control.

• 对于整合审计，在内部控制审计中获取的控制有效性的证据。

Assessing Control Risk

评估控制风险

32. The auditor should assess control risk for relevant assertions by evaluating the evidence obtained from all sources, including the auditor's testing of controls for the audit of internal control and the audit of financial statements, misstatements detected during the financial statement audit, and any identified control deficiencies.

32. 审计师应当通过评价所有来源获取的证据，包括内部控制审计和财务报表审计的控制测试、财务报表审计发现的错报和任何已识别的控制缺陷，评估相关认定的控制风险。

33. Control risk should be assessed at the maximum level for relevant assertions (1) for which controls necessary to sufficiently address the assessed risk of material misstatement in those assertions are missing or ineffective or (2) when the auditor has not obtained sufficient appropriate evidence to

33. 对于（1）控制缺失或失效的那些相关认定，而这些控制是充分处理其重大错报评定风险所必需的，或者（2）审计师没有获取充分适当的证据支持低于最大水平控制风险评估的

support a control risk assessment below the maximum level.

那些相关认定，控制风险应当评估为最高水平。

34. When deficiencies affecting the controls on which the auditor intends to rely are detected, the auditor should evaluate the severity of the deficiencies and the effect on the auditor′s control risk assessments. If the auditor plans to rely on controls relating to an assertion but the controls that the auditor tests are ineffective because of control deficiencies, the auditor should:

34. 当发现了审计师打算依赖的控制存在缺陷，审计师应当评价这些缺陷的严重性和对审计师的控制风险评估的影响。如果审计师计划依赖与某个认定相关的控制，但是由于控制缺陷，审计师测试的这些控制无效，审计师应当：

a. Perform tests of other controls related to the same assertion as the ineffective controls, or

a. 如同无效控制一样，实施与相同认定相关的其他控制测试，或

b. Revise the control risk assessment and modify the planned substantive procedures as necessary in light of the increased assessment of risk.

b. 按照提高的风险评估的需要，修订控制风险评估和修改预定实质性程序。

Note: Auditing Standard No. 5 establishes requirements for evaluating the severity of a control deficiency and communicating identified control deficiencies to management and the audit committee in an integrated audit. AU sec. 325, Communications About Control Deficiencies in an Audit of Financial Statements, establishes requirements for

注：审计准则第 5 号为整合审计中评价控制缺陷严重性和向管理层和审计委员会沟通制定要求。过渡审计准则第 325 条［在财务报表审计中对于控制缺陷的沟通］为仅有财务报表审计时对于重大缺陷和

communicating significant deficiencies and material weaknesses in an audit of financial statements only.

实质性弱点的沟通制定要求。

Testing Controls in an Audit of Internal Control
内部控制审计的控制测试

35. Auditing Standard No. 5 states that the objective of the tests of controls in an audit of internal control is to obtain evidence about the effectiveness of controls to support the auditor's opinion on the company's internal control over financial reporting. The auditor's opinion relates to the effectiveness of the company's internal control over financial reporting as of a point in time and taken as a whole. [17] Auditing Standard No. 5 establishes requirements regarding the selection of controls to be tested and the necessary nature, timing, and extent of tests of controls in an audit of internal control over financial reporting.

35. 审计准则第5号指出内部控制审计中控制测试的目标是获取控制有效性的证据，支持审计师对于公司财务报告内部控制的意见。审计师的意见与某一时点的公司财务报告内部控制有效性有关，并且作为一个整体看待。审计准则第5号为财务报告内部控制的受测控制的选取以及控制测试所需的性质、时间和范围制定要求。

Substantive Procedures
实质性程序

36. The auditor should perform substantive procedures for each relevant assertion of each significant account and disclosure, regardless

36. 审计师应当对每个重要账户和披露的每个相关认定实施实质性程序，而

of the assessed level of control risk.

不论控制风险的评定水平。

37. As the assessed risk of material misstatement increases, the evidence from substantive procedures that the auditor should obtain also increases. The evidence provided by the auditor's substantive procedures depends upon the mix of the nature, timing, and extent of those procedures. Further, for an individual assertion, different combinations of the nature, timing, and extent of testing might provide sufficient appropriate evidence to respond to the assessed risk of material misstatement.

37. 当评定的重大错报风险提高时，审计师从实质性程序获取的证据也需要增加。审计师的实质性程序提供的证据取决于这些程序的性质、时间和范围的组合。进一步而言，对于个别认定而言，测试的性质、时间和范围的不同组合可能提供与重大错报评定风险相对应的充分适当的证据。

38. Internal control over financial reporting has inherent limitations, [18] which, in turn, can affect the evidence that is needed from substantive procedures. For example, more evidence from substantive procedures ordinarily is needed for relevant assertions that have a higher susceptibility to management override or to lapses in judgment or breakdowns resulting from human failures. [19]

38. 财务报告内部控制有固有风险，反过来可能影响实质性程序所需的证据。例如，对于管理层凌驾于控制之上或人为故障导致的判断失误或崩溃而言具有较大敏感性的相关认定，需要从实质性程序获取更多证据。

Nature of Substantive Procedures
实质性程序的性质

39. Substantive procedures generally provide persuasive evidence when they are designed

39. 当实质性程序被设计和实施成获取相关和可靠

and performed to obtain evidence that is relevant and reliable. Also, some types of substantive procedures, by their nature, produce more persuasive evidence than others. Inquiry alone does not provide sufficient appropriate evidence to support a conclusion about a relevant assertion.

证据的时候，这些程序通常提供具有说服力的证据。另外，某些实质性程序类型从本质上讲提供比其他程序更有说服力的证据。询问本身不能提供充分适当的证据，用于支持某个相关认定的结论。

Note: Auditing Standard No. 15 discusses certain types of substantive procedures and the relevance and reliability of audit evidence.

注：审计准则第 15 号讨论实质性程序的某些类型和审计证据的相关性和可靠性。

40. Taking into account the types of potential misstatements in the relevant assertions that could result from identified risks, as required by paragraph 9. b. , can help the auditor determine the types and combination of substantive audit procedures that are necessary to detect material misstatements in the respective assertions.

40. 如同第 9. b. 款要求的，将已识别风险可能导致的相关认定的潜在错报的类型考虑在内，可以帮助审计师确定发现那些对应认定中的重大错报所需的实质性审计程序的类型和组合。

41. Substantive Procedures Related to the Period – end Financial Reporting Process. The auditor's substantive procedures must include the following audit procedures related to the period – end financial reporting process:

41. 与财务报告过程有关的实质性程序。审计师的实质性程序必须包括以下与期末财务报告过程有关的审计程序：

a. Reconciling the financial statements with

a. 将财务报表与构成其基

the underlying accounting records; and

础的会计记录相核对；和

b. Examining material adjustments made during the course of preparing the financial statements.

b. 检查编制财务报表期间所做的重大调整。

Note: AU secs. 316.58 – .62 establish requirements for examining journal entries and other adjustments for evidence of possible material misstatement due to fraud.

注：过渡审计准则第 316.58 至 .62 款对于检查会计分录和其他调整制定要求，以寻找舞弊可能导致的重大错报的证据。

Extent of Substantive Procedures

实质性程序的范围

42. The more extensively a substantive procedure is performed, the greater the evidence obtained from the procedure. The necessary extent of a substantive audit procedure depends on the materiality of the account or disclosure, the assessed risk of material misstatement, and the necessary degree of assurance from the procedure. However, increasing the extent of an audit procedure cannot adequately address an assessed risk of material misstatement unless the evidence to be obtained from the procedure is reliable and relevant.

42. 实施的实质性程序越广泛，该程序所获证据越多。实质性程序的必要范围取决于账户或披露的重要性、重大错报评定风险和需要从该程序获得的保证程度。但是，增加审计程序的范围不能充分处理重大错报评定风险，除非从该程序获得证据是可靠和相关的。

Timing of Substantive Procedures
实质性程序的时间

43. Performing certain substantive procedures at interim dates may permit early consideration of matters affecting the year - end financial statements, e. g. , testing material transactions involving higher risks of misstatement. However, performing substantive procedures at an interim date without performing procedures at a later date increases the risk that a material misstatement could exist in the year - end financial statements that would not be detected by the auditor. This risk increases as the period between the interim date and year end increases.

43. 在中期时点实施某些实质性程序可以较早地考虑影响期末财务报表的事项，比如，测试牵涉较高错报风险的重大交易。但是，在中期时点实施实质性程序而在更迟的时点不再实施程序，增加了年末财务报表存在重大错报的风险，而这些重大错报原本可以被审计师发现。中期时点与年末时点越远，该风险越大。

44. In determining whether it is appropriate to perform substantive procedures at an interim date, the auditor should take into account the following:

44. 确定在中期时点实施实质性程序是否适当时，审计师应当将以下事项考虑在内：

a. The assessed risk of material misstatement, including:

a. 重大错报评定风险，包括：

(1) The auditor's assessment of control risk, as discussed in paragraphs 32 - 34;

(1) 第32至34款讨论的审计师的控制风险评估；

(2) The existence of conditions or circumstances, if any, that create incentives or

(2) 存在在财务报表中期测试时点与期末之间诱

pressures on management to misstate the financial statements between the interim test date and the end of the period covered by the financial statements;

使或迫使管理层错报财务报表的状况或情况；

(3) The effects of known or expected changes in the company, its environment, or its internal control over financial reporting during the remaining period;

(3) 剩余期间在公司及其环境或财务报告内部控制方面已知或预计变化的影响；

b. The nature of the substantive procedures;

b. 实质性程序的性质；

c. The nature of the account or disclosure and relevant assertion; and

c. 账户或披露及其相关认定的性质；和

d. The ability of the auditor to perform the necessary audit procedures to cover the remaining period.

d. 审计师实施必要的审计程序涵盖剩余期间的能力。

45. When substantive procedures are performed at an interim date, the auditor should cover the remaining period by performing substantive procedures, or substantive procedures combined with tests of controls, that provide a reasonable basis for extending the audit conclusions from the interim date to the period end. Such procedures should include (a) comparing relevant information about the account balance at the interim date with comparable information at the end of the period

45. 如果中期时点实施了实质性程序，审计师应当对剩余期间实施实质性程序，或实质性程序与控制测试相结合，为将审计结论从中期时点延长到期末提供合理基础。这些程序应当包括（a）比较中期时点账户余额的相关资料与期末的可比资料，识别看起来异常的金额，并调

to identify amounts that appear unusual and investigating such amounts and (b) performing audit procedures to test the remaining period.

查这些金额，并且，(b) 实施审计程序，测试剩余期间。

46. If the auditor obtains evidence that contradicts the evidence on which the original risk assessments were based, including evidence of misstatements that he or she did not expect, the auditor should revise the related risk assessments and modify the planned nature, timing, or extent of substantive procedures covering the remaining period as necessary. Examples of such modifications include extending or repeating at the period end the procedures performed at the interim date.

46. 如果审计师取得的证据否定了初始风险评估所依据的证据，包括原先没有预料到的错报的证据，审计师应当修订相关风险评估，根据需要修改涵盖剩余期间预定实质性程序的性质、时间和范围。这些修改包括在期末延长或重复在中期时点实施的程序。

Dual - purpose Tests

双重目的测试

47. In some situations, the auditor might perform a substantive test of a transaction concurrently with a test of a control relevant to that transaction (a "dual - purpose test"). In those situations, the auditor should design the dual - purpose test to achieve the objectives of both the test of the control and the substantive test. Also, when performing a dual - purpose test, the auditor should evaluate the results of

47. 某些情况下，审计师可以在测试某个交易的控制的同时实施实质性程序（“双重目的测试”）。这些时候，审计师应当设计双重目的测试，同时达成控制测试和实质性程序的目标。另外，在实施双重目的测试时，审计师应当

the test in forming conclusions about both the assertion and the effectiveness of the control being tested. [20]

评价测试的结果，形成对于认定和受测控制的有效性二者的结论。

---

① See also paragraph .06 of AU sec. 230, Due Professional Care in the Performance of Work.

参见过渡审计准则第 230 条［业务实施中的职业审慎］第 .06 款。

② For integrated audits, paragraphs 61 and B13 of Auditing Standard No. 5, An Audit of Internal Control Over Financial Reporting That Is Integrated with An Audit of Financial Statements, establish requirements for introducing unpredictability in testing of controls from year to year and in multi – location audits.

对于整合审计，审计准则第 5 号［与财务报表审计合并执行的财务报告内部控制审计］第 61 和 B13 款为每年在控制测试和多场所审计中引入不可预见性制定要求。

③ Paragraphs 12 – 13 of Auditing Standard No. 12 discuss the auditor's responsibilities regarding obtaining an understanding of the company's selection and application of accounting principles. See also paragraphs .66 – .67 of AU sec. 316, Consideration of Fraud in a Financial Statement Audit, and paragraphs .04 and .06 of AU sec. 411, The Meaning of Present Fairly in Conformity With Generally Accepted Accounting Principles.

审计准则第 12 号第 12 至 13 款讨论审计师对于了解公司的会计政策选择和运用的责任。参见过渡审计准则第 316 条［财务报表审计中对于舞弊的考虑］第 .66 和 .67 款以及过渡审计准则第 411 条［遵循公认会计准则公允列报的含义］第 .04 和 .06 款。

④ AU secs. 230.07 – .09.

过渡审计准则第 230.07 至 .09 条

⑤ AU sec. 316.13.

过渡审计准则第 316.13 条

⑥ For example, potential misstatements regarding disclosures include omission of required disclosures or presentation of inaccurate or incomplete disclosures.

例如，与披露中包含遗漏规定的披露或列报不准确或不完整的披露有关的错报。

⑦ See paragraph 7. b. of Auditing Standard No. 8, Audit Risk, for a definition of control risk.

控制风险的定义参见审计准则第 8 号［审计风险］。

⑧ For purposes of this standard, the term "audit of financial statements" refers to the financial statement portion of the integrated audit and to the audit of financial statements only.

就本准则而言，“财务报表审计”是指整合审计的财务报表部分，以及财务报表审计本身。

⑨ Substantive procedures consist of (a) tests of details of accounts and disclosures and (b) substantive analytical procedures.

实质性程序包含（a）账户和披露的细节测试和（b）实质性分析程序。

⑩ See paragraph 71 of Auditing Standard No. 12 for factors that the auditor should evaluate in determining which risks are significant risks.

审计时在确定哪些风险是重大风险时应当评价的因素参见审计准则第 12 号第 71 款。

⑪ Paragraphs 14 – 15 of Auditing Standard No. 5.

审计准则第 5 号第 14 至 15 款。

⑫ Reliance on controls that is supported by sufficient and appropriate audit evidence allows the auditor to assess control risk at less than the maximum, which results in a lower assessed risk of material misstatement. In turn, this allows the auditor to modify the nature, timing, and extent of planned substantive procedures.

信赖由充分且适当的审计证据支持的控制允许审计师将控制风险评估为低于最高水平，获得较低的重大错报评定风险。因此，这使得审计师可以改变预定实质性程序的性质、时间和范围。

⑬ Terms defined in Appendix A, Definitions, are set in **boldface type** the first time they appear.

附录 A［定义］定义的用语首次出现时采用**粗体字**。

⑭ Paragraph 10 of Auditing Standard No. 15, Audit Evidence, and paragraph .16 of AU sec. 329, Substantive Analytical Procedures.

审计准则第 15 号［审计证据］第 10 款和过渡审计准则第 329 条［实质性分析程序］第 .16 款。

⑮ Paragraphs 37 – 38 of Auditing Standard No. 12 discuss performing a walkthrough.

审计准则第 12 号第 37 至 38 款讨论实施穿行测试。

⑯ The auditor also may use a benchmarking strategy, when appropriate, for automated application controls in subsequent years' audits. Benchmarking is described further beginning at paragraph B28 of Auditing Standard No. 5.

对于自动化应用控制，如果合适的话，在后续年度审计中，审计师还可以采用标杆策略。标杆策略从审计准则第 5 号第 B28 款开始有进一步的描述。

⑰ Paragraph B1 of Auditing Standard No. 5.

审计准则第 5 号第 B1 款。

⑱ Paragraph A5 of Auditing Standard No. 5.

审计准则第 5 号第 A5 款。

⑲ See, e. g., paragraph .14 of AU sec. 328, Auditing Fair Value Measurements and Disclosures.

参见过渡审计准则第 328 条［审计公允价值计量和披露］第 . 14 款。

⑳ Paragraph . 44 of AU sec. 350 discusses applying audit sampling in dual – purpose tests.

过渡审计准则第 350 条第 . 44 款讨论双重目的测试运用审计抽样。

Appendix A Definitions

附录A －定义

A1. For purposes of this standard, the terms listed below are defined as follows:

A1. 就本准则而言，以下用语的定义是：

A2. Dual – purpose test – Substantive test of a transaction and a test of a control relevant to that transaction that are performed concurrently, e. g. , a substantive test of sales transactions performed concurrently with a test of controls over those transactions.

A2. 双重目的测试：同时实施与某交易有关的实质性程序和控制测试，比如，销售交易的实质性程序与该交易的控制测试同时实施。

A3. Period of reliance – The period being covered by the company′s financial statements, or the portion of that period, for which the auditor plans to rely on controls in order to modify the nature, timing, and extent of planned substantive procedures.

A3. 信赖期间是审计师为了修改预定实质性程序的性质、时间和范围而打算依赖于控制的公司财务报表涵盖的期间或其一部分。

December 15, 2010
2010 年 12 月 15 日

AUDITING AND RELATED PROFESSIONAL PRACTICE STANDARDS
审计及相关专业实务准则

Auditing Standard No. 14 –
审计准则第 14 号 —

Evaluating Audit Results
评价审计结果

PCAOB

Public Company Accounting Oversight Board
公众公司会计监管委员会

[Effective pursuant to SEC Release No. 34 – 63606, File No. PCAOB – 2010 – 01, December 23, 2010]
[按照 SEC 第 34 – 63606 号公告生效；文件号：PCAOB – 2010 – 01，2012 年 12 月 23 日]

Final Rule: PCAOB Release No. 2010 – 004
最终规则：PCAOB 公告第 2010 – 004 号

Table of Contents

目　　录

Paragraph

款　　号

Introduction
引　言

1. This standard establishes requirements regarding the auditor's evaluation of audit results and determination of whether he or she has obtained sufficient appropriate audit evidence.

1. 本准则为审计师评价审计结果和确定是否获取了充分必要的审计证据制定要求。

Objective
目　标

2. The objective of the auditor is to evaluate the results of the audit to determine whether the audit evidence obtained is sufficient and appropriate to support the opinion to be expressed in the auditor's report.

2. 审计师的目标是评价审计结果确定所获审计证据对于支持审计报告将要发表的意见是否充分和适当。

Evaluating the Results of the Audit of Financial Statements
评价财务报表审计的结果

3. In forming an opinion on whether the financial statements are presented fairly, in all material respects, in conformity with the applicable financial reporting framework, the auditor should take into account all relevant audit evidence, regardless of whether it appears to corroborate or to contradict the assertions in the financial statements.

3. 在形成财务报表是否在所有重大方面遵循适用的财务报告框架公允列报的意见时，审计师应当考虑所有相关审计证据，而不论它看起来是否印证或否定财务报表的认定。

4. In the audit of financial statements,[①] the auditor's evaluation of audit results should include evaluation of the following:

4. 在财务报表审计中，审计师的审计结果评价应当包括下列事项的评价：

a. The results of analytical procedures performed in the overall review of the financial statements ("overall review");

a. 在财务报表总体审查（"总体审查"）中实施的分析性程序的结果；

b. Misstatements accumulated during the audit, including, in particular, uncorrected misstatements;[②]

b. 审计中的累计错报，尤其包括未纠正错报；

c. The qualitative aspects of the company's accounting practices;

c. 公司会计实务的质量方面；

d. Conditions identified during the audit that relate to the assessment of the risk of material misstatement due to fraud ("fraud risk");

d. 在审计中识别的与舞弊导致的重大错报风险（"舞弊风险"）评估有关的状况；

e. The presentation of the financial statements, including the disclosures; and

e. 财务报表的列报，包括披露；和

f. The sufficiency and appropriateness of the audit evidence obtained.

f. 获取的审计证据的充分性和适当性。

Performing Analytical Procedures in the Overall Review
在总体审查中实施分析性程序

5. In the overall review, the auditor should read the financial statements and disclosures and perform analytical procedures to (a) e-

5. 在总体审查中，审计师应当阅读财务报表和披露，并实施分析性程序，

valuate the auditor's conclusions formed regarding significant accounts and disclosures and (b) assist in forming an opinion on whether the financial statements as a whole are free of material misstatement.

以便（a）评价审计师形成的关于重要账户和披露的结论，和（b）帮助形成财务报表总体上没有重大错报的意见。

6. As part of the overall review, the auditor should evaluate whether:

6. 作为总体审查的一部分，审计师应当评价：

a. The evidence gathered in response to unusual or unexpected transactions, events, amounts, or relationships previously identified during the audit is sufficient; and

a. 针对审计中识别的非常规或非预期的交易、事件、金额或关系收集的证据是否充分；和

b. Unusual or unexpected transactions, events, amounts, or relationships[③] indicate risks of material misstatement that were not identified previously, including, in particular, fraud risks.

b. 非常规或非预期的交易、事件、金额或关系是否暗示原先未识别的重大错报风险，尤其是舞弊风险。

Note: If the auditor discovers a previously unidentified risk of material misstatement or concludes that the evidence gathered is not adequate, he or she should modify his or her audit procedures or perform additional procedures as necessary in accordance with paragraph 36 of this standard.

注：如果审计师发现了原先未识别的重大错报风险或认定收集的证据不充分，如有必要，应当遵照本准则第 36 款修改其审计程序或实施补充程序。

7. The nature and extent of the analytical procedures performed during the overall review may be similar to the analytical procedures performed as risk assessment proce-

7. 在总体审查中实施的分析性程序的性质和范围可以类似于风险评估程序中实施的分析性程序。审

dures. The auditor should perform analytical procedures relating to revenue through the end of the reporting period. ④

计师应当对整个报告期的收入实施有关的分析性程序。

8. The auditor should obtain corroboration for management's explanations regarding significant unusual or unexpected transactions, events, amounts, or relationships. If management's responses to the auditor's inquiries appear to be implausible, inconsistent with other audit evidence, imprecise, or not at a sufficient level of detail to be useful, the auditor should perform procedures to address the matter.

8. 审计师应当印证管理层对于重大非常规或非预期交易、事件、金额或关系的解释。如果管理层对于审计师询问的回答看起来不合理、与审计证据不一致、不精确或不能达到有用的详细程度，审计师应当实施程序来处理该事项。

9. Evaluating Whether Analytical Procedures Indicate a Previously Unrecognized Fraud Risk. Whether an unusual or unexpected transaction, event, amount, or relationship indicates a fraud risk, as discussed in paragraph 6. b. , depends on the relevant facts and circumstances, including the nature of the account or relationship among the data used in the analytical procedures. For example, certain unusual or unexpected transactions, events, amounts, or relationships could indicate a fraud risk if a component of the relationship involves accounts and disclosures that management has incentives or pressures to manipulate, e. g. , significant unusual or unexpected relationships involving revenue and income.

9. 评价分析性程序是否指向某个原先未识别的舞弊风险。非常规或非预期的交易、事件、金额或关系是否指向第 6. b 款讨论的舞弊风险取决于相关事实和具体情况，包括账户的性质或分析性程序所用数据之间的关系。例如，如果该关系的某个组成部分涉及管理层有意愿或被迫去操纵的账户或披露，比如，涉及收入和利润的重大非常规或非预期的关系，某些非常规或非预期的交易、事件、金额或关系可能指向某个舞弊风险。

Accumulating and Evaluating Identified Misstatements

累计和评价已识别的错报

10. Accumulating Identified Misstatements. The auditor should accumulate misstatements identified during the audit, other than those that are clearly trivial.

10. 累计已识别错报。审计师应当累计审计中识别的错报，除了那些明显的小差错。

Note: "Clearly trivial" is not another expression for "not material." Matters that are clearly trivial will be of a smaller order of magnitude than the materiality level established in accordance with Auditing Standard No. 11, Consideration of Materiality in Planning and Performing an Audit, and will be inconsequential, whether taken individually or in aggregate and whether judged by any criteria of size, nature, or circumstances. When there is any uncertainty about whether one or more items is clearly trivial, the matter is not considered trivial.

注："明显的小差错"并不是指"不重大"。明显的小差错是严重性程度小于遵循审计准则第 11 号［在计划和实施审计时对于重要性的考虑］制定的重要性的事项，并且无论个别还是合计，或者从大小、性质或具体情况等标准来看都不重要。如果对于某个或多个项目是否为小差错存在任何不确定性，那么，该事项就不能被认为是不重要的。

11. The auditor may designate an amount below which misstatements are clearly trivial and do not need to be accumulated. In such cases, the amount should be set so that any misstatements below that amount would not

11. 审计师可以指定一个金额，小于它的错报就是明显的小差错，并且无需累计。在这些情况下，该金额应当设定为，即使考

be material to the financial statements, individually or in combination with other misstatements, considering the possibility of undetected misstatement.

虑到未发现错报的可能性，低于该金额的任何错报，单独或与连同其他错报一起，对于财务报表而言也不是重大的。

12. The auditor's accumulation of misstatements should include the auditor's best estimate of the total misstatement in the accounts and disclosures that he or she has tested, not just the amount of misstatements specifically identified. This includes misstatements related to accounting estimates, as determined in accordance with paragraph 13 of this standard, and projected misstatements from substantive procedures that involve audit sampling, as determined in accordance with AU sec. 350, Audit Sampling. ⑤

12. 审计师的错报累计应当包括审计师在其已经测试的账户和披露中的错报合计的最佳估计，而不仅是明确识别的错报金额。这包括遵照本准则第 13 款确定的与会计估计有关的错报，以及来自涉及遵照过渡审计准则第 350 条［审计抽样］确定的审计抽样实质性程序的推断错报。

13. Misstatements Relating to Accounting Estimates. If the auditor concludes that the amount of an accounting estimate included in the financial statements is unreasonable or was not determined in conformity with the relevant requirements of the applicable financial reporting framework, he or she should treat the difference between that estimate and a reasonable estimate determined in conform-

13. 与会计估计有关的错报。如果审计师认定财务报表包含的会计估计的金额不合理或者没有遵照适当的财务报告框架的相关要求确定，审计师应当将该估计与遵照适当的会计政策确定的合理估计之间的差额看作错报。如果充

ity with the applicable accounting principles as a misstatement. If a range of reasonable estimates is supported by sufficient appropriate audit evidence and the recorded estimate is outside of the range of reasonable estimates, the auditor should treat the difference between the recorded accounting estimate and the closest reasonable estimate as a misstatement.

分适当的审计证据支持一定范围的合理估计，而且账面估计在合理估计范围之外，审计师应当将账面会计估计与最接近的合理估计之间的差额看作错报。

Note: If an accounting estimate is determined in conformity with the relevant requirements of the applicable financial reporting framework and the amount of the estimate is reasonable, a difference between an estimated amount best supported by the audit evidence and the recorded amount of the accounting estimate ordinarily would not be considered to be a misstatement. Paragraph 27 discusses evaluating accounting estimates for bias.

注：如果会计估计遵照适用的财务报告框架的相关要求确定，并且该估计的金额是合理的，由审计证据支持的最优估计金额与会计估计的账面金额之间的差额通常不被认为是错报。第 27 款讨论评价会计估计偏好。

14. Considerations as the Audit Progresses. The auditor should determine whether the overall audit strategy and audit plan need to be modified if:

14. 审计进行中的考虑。审计师应当确定总体审计策略和审计计划是否需要修改，如果：

a. The nature of accumulated misstatements

a. 累计错报的性质及其

and the circumstances of their occurrence indicate that other misstatements might exist that, in combination with accumulated misstatements, could be material; or

发生的具体情况表明可能存在其他错报，与累计错报合并，可能是重大的；或

b. The aggregate of misstatements accumulated during the audit approaches the materiality level or levels used in planning and performing the audit. ⑥

b. 审计中的累计错报的合计接近重要性或用于计划和实施审计的水平。

Note: When the aggregate of accumulated misstatements approaches the materiality level or levels used in planning and performing the audit, there likely will be greater than an appropriately low level of risk that possible undetected misstatements, when combined with the aggregate of misstatements accumulated during the audit that remain uncorrected, could be material to the financial statements. If the auditor's assessment of this risk is unacceptably high, he or she should perform additional audit procedures or determine that management has adjusted the financial statements so that the risk that the financial statements are materially misstated has been reduced to an appropriately low level.

注：当累计错报的合计接近重要性或用于计划和实施审计的水平，有可能存在大于适当的低水平的风险，即，可能的未发现错报，若与尚未纠正的审计中错报累计的合计合并，可能对于财务报表是重大的。如果审计师对此风险的评估是不可接受的高水平，应当实施补充审计程序或确定管理层已经调整财务报表，使得财务报表被重大错报已经被降到一个适当的低水平。

15. The auditor should communicate accumulated misstatements to management on a timely basis to provide management with an

15. 审计师应当向管理层及时沟通累计错报，使得管理层有机会纠正。

opportunity to correct them.

16. If management has examined an account or a disclosure in response to misstatements detected by the auditor and has made corrections to the account or disclosure, the auditor should evaluate management's work to determine whether the corrections have been recorded properly and whether uncorrected misstatements remain.

16. 如果管理层已经检查了某个账户或披露，作为对审计师发现错报的回应，并且已经纠正了账户或披露，审计师应当评价管理层的工作，确定该纠正是否已被适当地记账，以及未纠正错报是否仍然存在。

17. Evaluation of the Effect of Uncorrected Misstatements. The auditor should evaluate whether uncorrected misstatements are material, individually or in combination with other misstatements. In making this evaluation, the auditor should evaluate the misstatements in relation to the specific accounts and disclosures involved and to the financial statements as a whole, taking into account relevant quantitative and qualitative factors. ⑦ (See Appendix B.)

17. 评价未纠正错报的影响。审计师应当评价个别或连同其他错报一起的未纠正错报是否重大。在进行该评估时，审计师应当结合涉及的特定账户和披露以及财务报表整体评价重大错报，将相关的数量和质量因素考虑在内。（参见附录 B）

Note: In interpreting the federal securities laws, the Supreme Court of the United States has held that a fact is material if there is "a substantial likelihood that the …fact would have been viewed by the reasonable investor as having significantly altered the ' total

注：在解释美国联邦证券法律时，美国最高法院认为如果"理性投资者极有可能认为某事实已经显著改变了可用信息的'总体含义'"，那么，该事实

mix' of information made available." [8] As the Supreme Court has noted, determinations of materiality require "delicate assessments of the inferences a 'reasonable shareholder' would draw from a given set of facts and the significance of those inferences to him …" [9]

就是重要的。最高法院指出，重要性的确定需要"细致分析'理性投资者'从一组给定事实中可能得出的推论及其对于该投资者的重大性……"。

Note: As a result of the interaction of quantitative and qualitative considerations in materiality judgments, uncorrected misstatements of relatively small amounts could have a material effect on the financial statements. For example, an illegal payment of an otherwise immaterial amount could be material if there is a reasonable possibility[10] that it could lead to a material contingent liability or a material loss of revenue. [11] Also, a misstatement made intentionally could be material for qualitative reasons, even if relatively small in amount.

注：作为重要性判断中对于数量和质量相互影响的考虑，相对较小金额的未纠正错报可能对财务报表有重大影响。例如，某个不重大金额的非法付款可能是重大的，如果存在合理的可能性，它可能导致重大或有负债或重大收入损失。另外，故意的错报从质的理由来看可能是重大的，即使金额相对较小。

Note: If the reevaluation of the established materiality level or levels, as set forth in Auditing Standard No. 11, [12] results in a lower amount for the materiality level or levels, the auditor should take into account that lower materiality level or levels in the evaluation of uncorrected misstatements.

注：如果按照审计准则第 11 号规定的既定重要性的重新评价降低了重要性，审计师应当在评价未纠正错报时考虑这个更低的重要性。

18. The auditor's evaluation of uncorrected

18. 审计师按照本准则第

misstatements, as described in paragraph 17 of this standard, should include evaluation of the effects of uncorrected misstatements detected in prior years and misstatements detected in the current year that relate to prior years.

17 款对于未纠正错报的评价应当包括以前年度发现的未纠正错报的影响，以及与以前年度有关的本年发现的错报。

19. The auditor cannot assume that an instance of error or fraud is an isolated occurrence. Therefore, the auditor should evaluate the nature and effects of the individual misstatements accumulated during the audit on the assessed risks of material misstatement. This evaluation is important in determining whether the risk assessments remain appropriate, as discussed in paragraph 36 of this standard.

19. 审计师不能假设某个错误或舞弊是孤立的。因此，审计师应当评价个别错报的性质及其在审计中对于重大错报评定风险的累计影响。该评价对于确定本准则第 36 款讨论的风险评估是否仍然适当是重要的。

20. Evaluating Whether Misstatements Might Be Indicative of Fraud. The auditor should evaluate whether identified misstatements ⑬ might be indicative of fraud and , in turn , how they affect the auditor's evaluation of materiality and the related audit responses. As indicated in AU sec. 316, Consideration of Fraud in a Financial Statement Audit, fraud is an intentional act that results in material misstatement of the financial statements. ⑭

20. 评价错报是否可能暗示舞弊。审计师应当评价已识别错报是否可能暗示舞弊，并且，如何反过来影响审计师重要性的评价和相关的审计应对策略。如同过渡审计准则第 316 条［在财务报表审计中对于舞弊的考虑］所指出的，舞弊是一种导致财务报表重大错报的故意行为。

21. If the auditor believes that a misstatement

21. 如果审计师相信某个

is or might be intentional, and if the effect on the financial statements could be material or cannot be readily determined, the auditor should perform procedures to obtain additional audit evidence to determine whether fraud has occurred or is likely to have occurred and, if so, its effect on the financial statements and the auditor's report thereon.

错报是或可能是故意的，而且对于财务报表的影响可能是重大的或者不能轻易地确定，审计师应当实施程序获取补充审计证据，确定舞弊是否已发生或者有可能已发生，果真如此，那么它对于财务报表和审计报告的影响。

22. For misstatements that the auditor believes are or might be intentional, the auditor should evaluate the implications on the integrity of management or employees and the possible effect on other aspects of the audit. If the misstatement involves higher – level management, it might be indicative of a more pervasive problem, such as an issue with the integrity of management, even if the amount of the misstatement is small. In such circumstances, the auditor should reevaluate the assessment of fraud risk and the effect of that assessment on (a) the nature, timing, and extent of the necessary tests of accounts or disclosures and (b) the assessment of the effectiveness of controls. The auditor also should evaluate whether the circumstances or conditions indicate possible collusion involving employees, management, or external parties and, if so, the effect of the collusion

22. 对于审计师相信是或可能是故意的错报，审计师应当评价其对于管理层或员工诚信的含义，以及对于审计的其他方面的可能影响。如果该错报牵涉高层管理人员，它可能暗示更广泛的问题，即使错报金额较小。在这些情况下，审计师应当重新评价舞弊风险的评估和该评估对于（a）账户或披露所需的测试的性质、时间和范围以及（b）控制有效性评估的影响。审计师还应当评价这些情况或状况是否暗示员工、管理层或外部方面卷入可能的共谋，果真如此，那么共谋对于已获证据的可靠性的

on the reliability of evidence obtained.

影响。

23. If the auditor becomes aware of information indicating that fraud or another illegal act has occurred or might have occurred, he or she also must determine his or her responsibilities under AU secs. 316.79 – .82A, AU sec. 317, and Section 10A of the Securities Exchange Act of 1934, 15 U. S. C. § 78j – 1.

23. 如果审计师了解到已经发生或可能已经发生舞弊或其他非法行为的资料，审计师还必须根据过渡审计准则第 316.79 – .82A 条、过渡审计准则第 317 条和 1934 年美国证券交易法第 10A 条（15 U. S. C. § 78j – 1）确定其责任。

Evaluating the Qualitative Aspects of the Company's Accounting Practices

评价公司会计实务的质量方面

24. When evaluating whether the financial statements as a whole are free of material misstatement, the auditor should evaluate the qualitative aspects of the company's accounting practices, including potential bias in management's judgments about the amounts and disclosures in the financial statements.

24. 在评价财务报表总体是否没有重大错报时，审计师应当评价公司会计实务的质量方面，包括管理层对于财务报表金额和披露的判断的潜在偏好。

25. The following are examples of forms of management bias:

25. 以下是管理层偏好形式的举例：

a. The selective correction of misstatements brought to management's attention during the

a. 在审计中提交管理层的错报的选择性纠正（比

audit (e.g., correcting misstatements that have the effect of increasing reported earnings but not correcting misstatements that have the effect of decreasing reported earnings).

如，纠正那些具有增加盈利效果的错报，而不纠正那些具有减少盈利效果的错报）。

Note: To evaluate the potential effect of selective correction of misstatements, the auditor should obtain an understanding of the reasons that management decided not to correct misstatements communicated by the auditor in accordance with paragraph 15.

注：为了评价错报选择性纠正的潜在影响，审计师应当了解管理层决定不纠正审计师遵照第 15 款通报的错报的理由。

b. The identification by management of additional adjusting entries that offset misstatements accumulated by the auditor. If such adjusting entries are identified, the auditor should perform procedures to determine why the underlying misstatements were not identified previously and evaluate the implications on the integrity of management and the auditor's risk assessments, including fraud risk assessments. The auditor also should perform additional procedures as necessary to address the risk of further undetected misstatement.

b. 抵消审计师累计错报的管理层识别的补充调整分录。如果识别到这些调整分录，审计师应当实施程序确定上述错报原先没有被识别，并且评价其对于管理层诚信和审计师包括舞弊风险评估在内的风险评估的含义。审计师还应当实施必要的补充程序，处理进一步的未发现错报风险。

c. Bias in the selection and application of accounting principles. [15]

c. 在会计政策的选择和运用中的偏好。

d. Bias in accounting estimates. [16]

d. 在会计估计中的偏好。

26. If the auditor identifies bias in management's judgments about the amounts and disclosures in the financial statements, the auditor should evaluate whether the effect of that bias, together with the effect of uncorrected misstatements, results in material misstatement of the financial statements. Also, the auditor should evaluate whether the auditor's risk assessments, including, in particular, the assessment of fraud risks, and the related audit responses remain appropriate.

26. 如果审计师识别了管理层判断财务报表金额和披露的偏好，审计师应当评价该偏好的影响与未纠正错报合并，是否导致财务报表重大错报。另外，审计师应当评价包括舞弊风险评估在内的审计师的风险评估和相关审计应对策略是否仍然适当。

27. Evaluating Bias in Accounting Estimates. The auditor should evaluate whether the difference between estimates best supported by the audit evidence and estimates included in the financial statements, which are individually reasonable, indicate a possible bias on the part of the company's management. If each accounting estimate included in the financial statements was individually reasonable but the effect of the difference between each estimate and the estimate best supported by the audit evidence was to increase earnings or loss, the auditor should evaluate whether these circumstances indicate potential management bias in the estimates. Bias also can result from the cumulative effect of changes in multiple accounting estimates . If the estimates in the financial

27. 评价会计估计偏好。审计师应当评价被审计证据最佳支持的估计与财务报表包含的个别合理的估计之间的差额，是否暗示公司管理层方面可能的偏好。如果包含在财务报表中的该会计估计是个别合理的，但是每个估计与被审计证据最佳支持的估计之间差额的效果是增加盈利或亏损，审计师应当评价这些情况是否暗示管理层在这些估计中的偏好。偏好还会来自多个会计估计变更的累计影响。如果上一年的财务报表估计集中在合理估计范围的一

statements are grouped at one end of the range of reasonable estimates in the prior year and are grouped at the other end of the range of reasonable estimates in the current year, the auditor should evaluate whether management is using swings in estimates to achieve an expected or desired outcome, e. g. , to offset higher or lower than expected earnings.

端，而今年却在合理估计的另一端，审计师应当评价管理层是否利用估计的摇摆达到预期或理想的结果，比如，抵消较高或较低的预期收益。

Note: AU secs. 316. 64 – . 65 establish requirements regarding performing a retrospective review of accounting estimates and evaluating the potential for fraud risks.

注：过渡审计准则第316. 64 至 . 65 条为实施会计估计的追溯性审查和评价舞弊风险的潜在可能性制定要求。

Evaluating Conditions Relating to the Assessment of Fraud Risks

评价与舞弊风险评估相关的状况

28. When evaluating the results of the audit, the auditor should evaluate whether the accumulated results of auditing procedures[17] and other observations affect the assessment of the fraud risks made throughout the audit and whether the audit procedures need to be modified to respond to those risks. (See Appendix C.)

28. 在评价审计结果时，审计师应当评价审计程序的累计结果和其他发现是否影响贯穿审计过程的舞弊风险评估，以及为了应对这些风险，是否需要修改审计程序。（参见附录 C。）

29. As part of this evaluation, the engage-

29. 作为本评价的一部

ment partner should determine whether there has been appropriate communication with the other engagement team members throughout the audit regarding information or conditions that are indicative of fraud risks.

分，业务合伙人应当确定是否在审计全过程中与业务团队其他成员沟通暗示舞弊风险的资料或状况。

Note: To accomplish this communication, the engagement partner might arrange another discussion among the engagement team members about fraud risks. (See paragraphs 49 – 51 of Auditing Standard No. 12.)

注:为了实现本沟通,业务合伙人可以安排另一次业务团队成员之间对于舞弊风险的讨论。(参见审计准则第 12 号第 49 至 51 条。)

Evaluating the Presentation of the Financial Statements, Including the Disclosures

评价包括披露在内的财务报表列报

30. The auditor must evaluate whether the financial statements are presented fairly, in all material respects, in conformity with the applicable financial reporting framework.

30. 审计师必须评价财务报表是否在所有重大方面遵循适当的财务报告框架列报。

Note: AU sec. 411, The Meaning of Present Fairly in Conformity With Generally Accepted Accounting Principles, establishes requirements for evaluating the presentation of the financial statements. Auditing Standard No. 6, Evaluating Consistency of Financial Statements, establishes requirements regarding evaluating the consistency of the accounting principles used in financial statements.

注：过渡审计准则第 411 条［遵循公认会计准则公允列报的含义］为评价财务报表列报制定要求。审计准则第 6 号［评价财务报表的一致性］为评价财务报表采用的会计政策的一致性制定要求。

Note: The auditor should look to the requirements of the Securities and Exchange Commission for the company under audit with respect to the accounting principles applicable to that company.

注：审计师应当留意美国证券交易委员会对于被审计公司适用的会计政策的要求。

31. As part of the evaluation of the presentation of the financial statements, the auditor should evaluate whether the financial statements contain the information essential for a fair presentation of the financial statements in conformity with the applicable financial reporting framework. Evaluation of the information disclosed in the financial statements includes consideration of the form, arrangement, and content of the financial statements (including the accompanying notes), encompassing matters such as the terminology used, the amount of detail given, the classification of items in the statements, and the bases of amounts set forth.

31. 作为财务报表列报评价的一部分，审计师应当评价财务报表是否包含遵循适当的财务报告框架的财务报表公允列报所必备的资料。评价财务报表披露的资料包括财务报表（包括报表附注）的形式、安排和内容等方面的考虑，涵盖诸如术语的运用、显示细节的数量、报表项目的分类和上述金额的列报基础等事项。

Note: According to AU sec. 508, if the financial statements, including the accompanying notes, fail to disclose information that is required by the applicable financial reporting framework, the auditor should express a qualified or adverse opinion and should provide the information in the report, if practicable , unless its omission from the report is

注：根据过渡审计准则第 508 条，财务报表及其附注如果不能披露适用的财务报告框架规定的资料，审计师应当发表有保留或否定意见，并且，如果可行的话，应当在报告中提供该资料，除非报告不提

recognized as appropriate by a specific auditing standard. [18]

供该资料是被特定审计准则认为适当的。

Evaluating the Sufficiency and Appropriateness of Audit Evidence

评价审计证据的充分性和适当性

32. Auditing Standard No. 8, Audit Risk, states:

32. 审计准则第 8 号［审计风险］指出：

To form an appropriate basis for expressing an opinion on the financial statements, the auditor must plan and perform the audit to obtain reasonable assurance about whether the financial statements are free of material misstatement due to error or fraud. Reasonable assurance is obtained by reducing audit risk to an appropriately low level through applying due professional care, including obtaining sufficient appropriate audit evidence. [19]

为了形成发表财务报表审计意见的适当基础，审计师必须计划和实施审计，获取有关财务报表没有错误或舞弊导致的重大错报的合理保证。合理保证是通过运用包括获取充分适当的审计证据在内的职业审慎将审计风险降到适当的低水平而获得的。

33. As part of evaluating audit results, the auditor must conclude on whether sufficient appropriate audit evidence has been obtained to support his or her opinion on the financial statements.

33. 作为评价审计结果的一部分，审计师必须对是否已获取支持其财务报表意见的充分适当的审计证据得出结论。

34. Factors that are relevant to the conclusion on whether sufficient appropriate audit evidence has been obtained include the following:

34. 与是否已获取充分适当审计证据的结论有关的因素包括：

a. The significance of uncorrected misstatements and the likelihood of their having a material effect, individually or in combination, on the financial statements, considering the possibility of further undetected misstatement (paragraphs 14 and 17 – 19 of this standard).

a. 在考虑到更多未发现错报的可能性的情况下，未纠正错报的重大性和它们个别或连同其他错报一起，对于财务报表有重大影响的可能性（本准则第17至19款）。

b. The results of audit procedures performed in the audit of financial statements, including whether the evidence obtained supports or contradicts management's assertions and whether such audit procedures identified specific instances of fraud (paragraphs 20 – 23 and 28 – 29 of this standard).

b. 在财务报表审计中实施的审计程序的结果，包括获取的证据是否支持或否定管理层的认定，并且，这些审计程序是否识别特定的舞弊情况（本准则第20至23和28至29款）。

c. The auditor's risk assessments (paragraph 36 of this standard).

c. 审计师的风险评估（本准则第36款）。

d. The results of audit procedures performed in the audit of internal control over financial reporting, if the audit is an integrated audit.

d. 如果该审计是整合审计的话，财务报告内部控制审计中实施的审计程序的结果。

e. The appropriateness (i. e., the relevance and reliability) of the audit evidence obtained. [20]

e. 获得的审计证据的适当性（即相关性和可靠性）。

35. If the auditor has not obtained sufficient appropriate audit evidence about a relevant

35. 如果审计师没有获取相关认定的充分适当的审

assertion or has substantial doubt about a relevant assertion, the auditor should perform procedures to obtain further audit evidence to address the matter. If the auditor is unable to obtain sufficient appropriate audit evidence to have a reasonable basis to conclude about whether the financial statements as a whole are free of material misstatement, AU sec. 508 indicates that the auditor should express a qualified opinion or a disclaimer of opinion. [21]

计证据或者严重怀疑某个相关认定，审计师应当实施程序获取进一步的审计证据来处理该事项。如果审计师不能获取充分适当的审计证据为决定财务报表总体上没有重大错报获得合理的基础，过渡审计准则第 508 条指出审计师应当发表有保留意见或拒绝表示意见。

36. Evaluating the Appropriateness of Risk Assessments. As part of the evaluation of whether sufficient appropriate audit evidence has been obtained, the auditor should evaluate whether the assessments of the risks of material misstatement at the assertion level remain appropriate and whether the audit procedures need to be modified or additional procedures need to be performed as a result of any changes in the risk assessments. For example, the re – evaluation of the auditor′s risk assessments could result in the identification of relevant assertions or significant risks that were not identified previously and for which the auditor should perform additional audit procedures.

36. 评价审计评估的适当性。作为评价是否已获取充分适当的审计证据的一部分，审计师应当评价认定层次的重大错报风险的评估是否仍然适当，以及作为风险评估改变的结果，审计程序是否需要修改或者需要执行补充审计程序。例如，审计师的风险评估的重新评价可能导致识别原先没有被识别的相关认定或重大风险，并且，审计师应当为此实施补充审计程序。

Note : Auditing Standard No . 1 2 establishes

注：审计准则第 12 号为

requirements on revising the auditor's risk assessment. ㉒ Auditing Standard No. 13 discusses the auditor's responsibilities regarding the assessment of control risk and evaluation of control deficiencies in an audit of financial statements. ㉓

修改审计师的风险评估制定要求。审计准则第13号讨论审计师在财务报表审计中对于控制风险评估和控制缺陷评价的责任。

Evaluating the Results of the Audit of Internal Control Over Financial Reporting
评价财务报告内部控制审计的结果

37. Auditing Standard No. 5, An Audit of Internal Control Over Financial Reporting That Is Integrated with An Audit of Financial Statements, indicates that the auditor should form an opinion on the effectiveness of internal control over financial reporting by evaluating evidence obtained from all sources, including the auditor's testing of controls, misstatements detected during the financial statement audit, and any identified control deficiencies. Auditing Standard No. 5 describes the auditor's responsibilities regarding evaluating the results of the audit, including evaluating the identified control deficiencies. ㉔

37. 审计准则第5号［与财务报表审计合并执行的财务报告内部控制审计］指出审计师应当通过评价从所有来源取得的证据，包括审计师的控制测试、财务报表审计中发现的错报和任何已识别的控制缺陷，形成关于财务报告内部控制有效性的意见。审计准则第5号规定了审计师对于评价审计结果的责任，包括评价已识别的控制缺陷。

① For purposes of this standard, the term "audit of financial statements" refers to the financial statement portion of the integrated audit and to the audit of financial statements only.

就本准则而言，“财务报表审计”是指整合审计的财务报表部分以及财务报表审计本身。

② Terms defined in Appendix A, Definitions, are set in **boldface type** the first time they appear.

附录 A［定义］定义的用语首次出现时采用**粗体字**。

③ Paragraphs 46 – 48 of Auditing Standard No. 12, Identifying and Assessing Risks of Material Misstatement and paragraph .03 of AU sec. 329, Substantive Analytical Procedures.

审计准则第 12 号［识别和评估重大错报风险］第 46 至 48 款和过渡审计准则第 329 条［实质性分析程序］第 .03 款。

④ Paragraph 47 of Auditing Standard No. 12 contains a requirement to perform analytical procedures relating to revenue as part of the risk assessment procedures.

审计程序第 12 号第 47 款包含了实施与收入有关的作为风险评估程序一部分的分析性复核的要求。

⑤ AU sec. 350.26.

过渡审计准则第 350.26 条

⑥ Auditing Standard No. 11.

审计准则第 11 号。

⑦ If the financial statements contain material misstatements, AU sec. 508, Reports on Audited Financial Statements, indicates that the auditor should issue a qualified or an adverse opinion on the financial statements. AU sec. 508.35 discusses situations in which the financial statements are materially affected by a departure from the applicable financial reporting framework.

如果财务报表有重大错报，过渡审计准则第 508 条［报告经审计财务报表］指出审计师应当对财务报表发表有保留或否定意见。过渡审计准则第 508.35 条讨论财务报表由于违背适用的财务报告框架受到重大影响的情况。

⑧ TSC Industries v. Northway, Inc., 426 U.S. 438, 449 (1976). See also Basic, Inc. v. Levinson, 485 U.S. 224 (1988).

TSC Industries 诉 Northway, Inc., 426 U.S. 438, 449 (1976)。参见 Basic, Inc. 诉 Levinson, 485 U.S. 224 (1988)。

⑨ TSC Industries, 426 U.S. at 450.

TSC 工业公司, 426 U.S. at 450。

⑩ There is a reasonable possibility of an event, as used in this standard, when the likelihood of the event is either "reasonably possible" or "probable," as those terms are used in the FASB Accounting Standards Codification, Contingencies Topic, paragraph 450 – 20 – 25 – 1.

本准则所称某事件存在合理的可能性是指该事件的发生要么“合理的可能”，要么“有可能”，这两个词汇的定义与美国财务会计准则委员会“会计准则汇编”［或有事项］第 450 – 20 – 25 – 1 款的定义一致。

⑪ AU sec. 317, Illegal Acts by Clients.

过渡审计准则第 317 条［客户的非法行为］

⑫ Paragraphs 11 – 12 of Auditing Standard No. 11.

审计准则第 11 号第 11 至 12 款。

⑬ Misstatements include omission and presentation of inaccurate or incomplete disclosures.

错报包括遗漏和不准确或不完整的披露的列报。

⑭ AU sec. 316. 05.

过渡审计准则第 316. 05 条。

⑮ Paragraph 5. d. of Auditing Standard No. 13, The auditor's Responses to the Risks of Material Misstatement.

审计准则第 13 号［审计师对于重大错报风险的应对策略］第 5. d. 款。

⑯ Paragraph 27 of this standard.

本准则第 27 款。

⑰ Such auditing procedures include, but are not limited to, procedures in the overall review (paragraph 9 of this standard), the evaluation of identified misstatements (paragraphs 20 – 23 of this standard), and the evaluation of the qualitative aspects of the company's accounting practices (paragraphs 24 – 27 of this standard).

这些审计程序包括，但不限于，总体审查程序（本准则第 9 款）、已识别错报的评价（本准则第 20 至 23 款）和公司会计实务质量方面的评价（本准则第 24 至 27 款）。

⑱ AU secs. 508. 41 – . 44.

过渡审计准则第 508. 41 至 . 44 条。

⑲ Paragraph 3 of Auditing Standard No. 8.

审计准则第 8 号第 3 款。

⑳ Paragraphs 7 – 9 of Auditing Standard No. 15, Audit Evidence, discuss the relevance and reliability of audit evidence.

审计准则第 15 号［审计证据］第 7 至 9 款讨论审计证据的相关性和可靠性。

㉑ AU sec. 508. 22 – . 34 contains requirements regarding audit scope limitations.

过渡审计准则第 508. 22 至 . 34 款包含对于审计范围限制的要求。

㉒ Paragraph 74 of Auditing Standard No. 12.

审计准则第 12 号第 74 款。

㉓ Paragraphs 32 – 34 of Auditing Standard No. 13.

审计准则第 13 号第 32 至 34 款。

㉔ Paragraphs 62 – 70 of Auditing Standard No. 5 discuss evaluating identified control deficiencies, and paragraphs 71 – 73 of Auditing Standard No. 5 discuss forming an opinion on the effectiveness of internal control over financial reporting.

审计准则第 5 号第 62 至 70 款讨论评价已识别的控制缺陷，审计准则第 5 号第 71 至 73 款讨论形成财务报告内部控制有效性的审计意见。

Appendix A Definitions

附录A - 定义

A1. For purposes of this standard, the terms listed below are defined as follows:

A1. 就本准则而言，以下用语的定义是：

A2. Misstatement - A misstatement, if material individually or in combination with other misstatements, causes the financial statements not to be presented fairly in conformity with the applicable financial reporting framework. ① A misstatement may relate to a difference between the amount, classification, presentation, or disclosure of a reported financial statement item and the amount, classification, presentation, or disclosure that should be reported in conformity with the applicable financial reporting framework. Misstatements can arise from error (i. e., unintentional misstatement) or fraud. ②

A2. 错报：单独或连同其他错报一起的重大错报导致财务报表没有遵循适用的财务报告框架公允地列报。错报可能与报出的财务报表项目的金额、分类、列报或披露与遵循适用的财务报表框架应当报出的金额、分类、列报或披露的差别有关。错报可以源自错误（即无心的错报）或舞弊。

A3. Uncorrected misstatements - Misstatements, other than those that are clearly trivial, ③ that management has not corrected.

A3. 未纠正错报：除了明显的小差错，管理层尚未纠正的那些错报。

---

① The auditor should look to the requirements of the Securities and Exchange Commission for the company under audit with respect to the accounting principles applicable to that company.
审计师应当留意美国证券交易委员会关于该被审计公司所适用的会计政策的有关要求。

② Paragraph .02 of AU sec. 316, Consideration of Fraud in a Financial Statement Audit.
过渡审计准则第 316 条［在财务报表审计中对于舞弊的考虑］第 .02 款。

③ Paragraph 10 of this standard states that, "[t] he auditor should accumulate misstatements identified during the audit, other than those that are clearly trivial."
本准则第 10 款指出"审计师应当累计审计中识别的错报，除了那些明显的小差错。"

Appendix B Qualitative Factors Related to the Evaluation of the Materiality of Uncorrected Misstatements
附录B－与未纠正错报的重要性评价有关的质量因素

B1. Paragraph 17 of this standard states:

B1. 本准则第 17 款指出：

The auditor should evaluate whether uncorrected misstatements are material, individually or in combination with other misstatements. In making this evaluation, the auditor should evaluate the misstatements in relation to the specific accounts and disclosures involved and to the financial statements as a whole, taking into account relevant quantitative and qualitative factors. ①

审计师应当评价未纠正错报，单独或连同其他错报一起，是否重大。在做出该评价时，审计师应当结合涉及的特定账户或披露以及财务报表总体进行评价，考虑相关的数量和质量因素。

Note: In interpreting the federal securities laws, the Supreme Court of the United States has held that a fact is material if there is "a substantial likelihood that the …fact would have been viewed by the reasonable investor as having significantly altered the 'total mix' of information made available." ② As the Supreme Court has noted, determinations of materiality require "delicate assessments of the inferences a 'reasonable shareholder'

注：在解释美国联邦证券法律时，美国最高法院认为如果"理性投资者极有可能认为某事实已经显著改变了可用信息的'总体含义'"，那么，该事实就是重要的。最高法院指出，重要性的确定需要"细致分析'理性投资者'从一组给定事实中可

would draw from a given set of facts and the significance of those inferences to him …" [3]

能得出的推论及其对于该投资者的重大性……"

Note: As a result of the interaction of quantitative and qualitative considerations in materiality judgments, uncorrected misstatements of relatively small amounts could have a material effect on the financial statements. For example, an illegal payment of an otherwise immaterial amount could be material if there is a reasonable possibility[4] that it could lead to a material contingent liability or a material loss of revenue. [5] Also, a misstatement made intentionally could be material for qualitative reasons, even if relatively small in amount.

注：作为重要性判断中对于数量和质量的相互影响的考虑，相对较小金额的未纠正错报可能对财务报表有重大影响。例如，某个不重大金额的非法付款可能是重大的，如果存在合理的可能性，它可能导致重大或有负债或重大收入损失。另外，故意的错报从质的理由来看可能是重大的，即使金额相对较小。

B2. Qualitative factors to consider in the auditor's evaluation of the materiality of uncorrected misstatements, if relevant, include the following:

B2. 在审计师评价未纠正错报时考虑的质量因素包括：

a. The potential effect of the misstatement on trends, especially trends in profitability.

a. 该错报对于趋势的潜在影响，尤其是利润率趋势。

b. A misstatement that changes a loss into income or vice versa.

b. 将亏损变为盈利的某个错报，后者正相反。

c. The effect of the misstatement on segment information, for example, the significance of

c. 错报对于分部资料的影响，比如，该事件对于某

the matter to a particular segment important to the future profitability of the company, the pervasiveness of the matter on the segment information, and the impact of the matter on trends in segment information, all in relation to the financial statements taken as a whole.

个对公司未来盈利性而言重要的特定分部的重大性，该事件对于分部资料的广泛性，以及该事项对于分部资料的趋势的影响，全部与财务报表整体有关。

d. The potential effect of the misstatement on the company's compliance with loan covenants, other contractual agreements, and regulatory provisions.

d. 错报对于公司遵守贷款协议、其他契约性协议和监管规定的潜在影响。

e. The existence of statutory or regulatory reporting requirements that affect materiality thresholds.

e. 存在影响重要性门槛的法律或监管报告要求。

f. A misstatement that has the effect of increasing management's compensation, for example, by satisfying the requirements for the award of bonuses or other forms of incentive compensation.

f. 具有增加管理层薪酬效果的错报，例如，满足奖金发放或其他形式的激励性薪酬的要求。

g. The sensitivity of the circumstances surrounding the misstatement, for example, the implications of misstatements involving fraud and possible illegal acts, violations of contractual provisions, and conflicts of interest.

g. 该错报所处环境的敏感性，例如，错报暗示涉及舞弊和可能的非法行为、违反契约性条款和利益冲突等。

h. The significance of the financial statement element affected by the misstatement , for ex-

h. 受到错报影响的财务报表要素的重大性，例

ample, a misstatement affecting recurring earnings as contrasted to one involving a non-recurring charge or credit, such as an extraordinary item.

如，影响经常性利润的错报相对于涉及非经常性费用或冲销的错报，比如，非经常性项目。

i. The effects of misclassifications, for example, misclassification between operating and non-operating income or recurring and non-recurring income items.

i. 错误分类的影响，例如，经营和非经营收入的错误分类，或者，经常性和非经常性收入项目的错误分类。

j. The significance of the misstatement or disclosures relative to known user needs, for example:

j. 该错报或披露相对于已知使用者需要的重大性，例如：

- The significance of earnings and earnings per share to public company investors.

- 利润和每股收益对于公众公司投资者的重大性。

- The magnifying effects of a misstatement on the calculation of purchase price in a transfer of interests (buy/sell agreement).

- 利益转移（买/卖协议）中计算购买价格时重大错报的放大效果。

- The effect of misstatements of earnings when contrasted with expectations.

- 利润与预期对比时错报的影响。

k. The definitive character of the misstatement, for example, the precision of an error that is objectively determinable as contrasted with a misstatement that unavoidably involves a degree of subjectivity through estimation,

k. 错报的确定性属性，例如，可以客观确定准确度的某个错误相对于不可避免地涉及某种程度的主观性的估计、分配或不确

allocation, or uncertainty.

定性的错报。

l. The motivation of management with respect to the misstatement, for example, (i) an indication of a possible pattern of bias by management when developing and accumulating accounting estimates or (ii) a misstatement precipitated by management's continued unwillingness to correct weaknesses in the financial reporting process.

l. 与该错报有关的管理层的动机，例如，（1）管理层在准备和累计会计估计时可能的偏见模式，和（2）由于管理层始终不愿纠正财务报告过程的弱点促成的错报。

m. The existence of offsetting effects of individually significant but different misstatements.

m. 个别重大但不同错报的抵消效果的存在。

n. The likelihood that a misstatement that is currently immaterial may have a material effect in future periods because of a cumulative effect, for example, that builds over several periods.

n. 当前不重大的错报由于累积效应在未来期间有重大影响的可能性，例如，经过数个期间的积累。

o. The cost of making the correction ? it may not be cost - beneficial for the client to develop a system to calculate a basis to record the effect of an immaterial misstatement. On the other hand, if management appears to have developed a system to calculate an amount that represents an immaterial misstatement, it may reflect a motivation of management as noted in paragraph B2. l above.

o. 纠正的成本:对于客户而言,开发一个系统用于计算登记非重大错报影响的基础可能不划算。另一方面,如果管理层看起来已经开发了一个系统用于计算某个代表非重大错报的金额,它也许反映了上面B2 款提到的管理层动机。

p. The risk that possible additional undetected misstatements would affect the auditor's evaluation.

p. 可能的更多的未发现错报可能影响审计师评价的风险。

① If the financial statements contain material misstatements, AU sec. 508, Reports on Audited Financial Statements, indicates that the auditor should issue a qualified or an adverse opinion on the financial statements. AU sec. 508.35 discusses situations in which the financial statements are materially affected by a departure from the applicable financial reporting framework.

如果财务报表包含重大错报，过渡审计准则第 508 条［报告经审计财务报表］指出审计师应当对该财务报表发表有保留意见或否定意见。过渡审计准则第 508.35 条讨论财务报表由于违背适用的财务报告框架受到重大影响的情况。

② TSC Industries v. Northway, Inc., 426 U.S. 438, 449 (1976). See also Basic, Inc. v. Levinson, 485 U.S. 224 (1988).

TSC Industries 诉 Northway, Inc., 426 U.S. 438, 449 (1976)。参见 Basic, Inc. 诉 Levinson, 485 U.S. 224 (1988)。

③ TSC Industries, 426 U.S. at 450.

TSC 工业公司, 426 U.S. at 450。

④ There is a reasonable possibility of an event, as used in this standard, when the likelihood of the event is either "reasonably possible" or "probable," as those terms are used in the FASB Accounting Standards Codification, Contingencies Topic, paragraph 450-20-25-1.

本准则所称某事件存在合理的可能性是指该事件的发生要么"合理的可能"，要么"有可能"，这两个词汇的定义与美国财务会计准则委员会"会计准则汇编"［或有事项］第 450-20-25-1 款的定义一致。

⑤ AU sec. 317, Illegal Acts by Clients.

过渡审计准则第 317 条［客户的非法行为］

Appendix C Matters That Might Affect the Assessment of Fraud Risks

附录C －可能影响舞弊风险评估的事项

C1. If the following matters are identified

C1. 如果在审计中识别到

during the audit, the auditor should take into account these matters in the evaluation of the assessment of fraud risks, as discussed in paragraph 28 of this standard:

下列事项，审计师应当如本准则第 28 款讨论的那样，在舞弊风险评估的评价中将这些事项考虑在内：

a. Discrepancies in the accounting records, including:

a. 会计记录中的差异，包括：

(1) Transactions that are not recorded in a complete or timely manner or are improperly recorded as to amount, accounting period, classification, or company policy.

(1) 没有完整或及时登记的交易，或者，在金额、会计期间、分类或公司政策等方面不适当地登记。

(2) Unsupported or unauthorized balances or transactions.

(2) 没有依据的或未经授权的余额或交易。

(3) Last - minute adjustments that significantly affect financial results.

(3) 显著影响财务成果的最后一分钟的调整。

(4) Evidence of employees' access to systems and records that is inconsistent with the access that is necessary to perform their authorized duties.

(4) 员工访问系统或记录的证据，而该访问与履行其受权职责所需的访问不相符。

(5) Tips or complaints to the auditor about alleged fraud.

(5) 审计师收到的关于被告发的舞弊的举报或投诉。

b. Conflicting or missing evidence, including:

b. 相互矛盾或缺失的证据，包括：

(1) Missing documents.

(1) 缺失文档。

(2) Documents that appear to have been altered. ①

(2) 看起来已经被变造的文档。

(3) Unavailability of other than photocopied or electronically transmitted documents when documents in original form are expected to exist.

(3) 文档的原始形式预期存在，但是只能取得复印件或电子传输的文档。

(4) Significant unexplained items in reconciliations.

(4) 调节中重大的未作解释的项目。

(5) Inconsistent, vague, or implausible responses from management or employees arising from inquiries or analytical procedures.

(5) 询问或分析性程序得到来自管理层或员工的不一致、模糊或不合理的回答。

(6) Unusual discrepancies between the company's records and confirmation responses.

(6) 公司记录与函证回复之间不寻常的差异。

(7) Missing inventory or physical assets of significant magnitude.

(7) 大量存货或实物资产的遗失。

(8) Unavailable or missing electronic evidence that is inconsistent with the company's record retention practices or policies.

(8) 没有或缺失电子证据，不符合公司的记录留存实务或政策。

(9) Inability to produce evidence of key

(9) 不能提供关键系统

systems development and program change testing and implementation activities for current year system changes and deployments.

的开发和程序变更测试、当年系统变更和投入使用的实施活动的证据。

(10) Unusual balance sheet changes or changes in trends or important financial statement ratios or relationships, e. g. , receivables growing faster than revenues.

(10) 不寻常的资产负债表变动、在趋势或重要财务报表比率或关系方面的变动，比如，应收账款增长快于收入增长。

(11) Large numbers of credit entries and other adjustments made to accounts receivable records.

(11) 在应收账款记录中存在大量贷方分录和其他调整。

(12) Unexplained or inadequately explained differences between the accounts receivable subsidiary ledger and the general ledger control account, or between the customer statement and the accounts receivable subsidiary ledger.

(12) 未作解释或解释不充分的在应收账款明细账与总账控制账户之间的差额，或者，在客户声明和应收账款明细账之间的差额。

(13) Missing or nonexistent cancelled checks in circumstances in which cancelled checks are ordinarily returned to the company with the bank statement.

(13) 缺失或不存在注销的支票，而实际情况是注销的支票通常与银行对账单一起被退回公司。

(14) Fewer responses to confirmation requests than anticipated or a greater number

(14) 少于预期的函证回复或者大于预期数量的回

of responses than anticipated.

复。

c. Problematic or unusual relationships between the auditor and management, including:

c. 审计师与管理层之间不易相处或不同寻常的关系包括：

(1) Denial of access to records, facilities, certain employees, customers, vendors, or others from whom audit evidence might be sought, including: ②

(1) 拒绝审计师接触记录、设施、某些员工、客户、供应商或其他可能被寻求审计证据的人员，包括：

• Unwillingness to facilitate auditor access to key electronic files for testing through the use of computer – assisted audit techniques.

• 不愿协助审计师为了通过利用计算机辅助审计技术进行测试而接触关键电子文件；

• Denial of access to key information technology operations staff and facilities, including security, operations, and systems development.

• 拒绝审计师接触关键信息技术运行人员和设施，包括安全、运行和系统开发人员。

(2) Undue time pressures imposed by management to resolve complex or contentious issues.

(2) 管理层对于解决复杂或有争议事项施加不可承受的时间压力。

(3) Management pressure on engagement team members, particularly in connection with the auditor's critical assessment of audit

(3) 管理层对于业务团队成员的压力，尤其是与审计师审计证据的关键评

evidence or in the resolution of potential disagreements with management.

估或者解决与管理层的潜在不一致等相关方面。

(4) Unusual delays by management in providing requested information.

(4) 管理层提交所需资料的不寻常的延误。

(5) Management's unwillingness to add or revise disclosures in the financial statements to make them more complete and transparent.

(5) 管理层不愿增加或修改财务报表披露，使其更完整和透明。

(6) Management's unwillingness to appropriately address significant deficiencies in internal control on a timely basis.

(6) 管理层不愿及时适当地处理内部控制的重大缺陷。

d. Other matters, including:

d. 其他事项，包括：

(1) Objections by management to the auditor meeting privately with the audit committee.

(1) 管理层拒绝审计师单独与审计委员会会面。

(2) Accounting policies that appear inconsistent with industry practices that are widely recognized and prevalent.

(2) 会计政策与广泛认可和优先采用的行业实务看起来不一致。

(3) Frequent changes in accounting estimates that do not appear to result from changing circumstances.

(3) 会计估计的频繁变动看起来不是源于环境的变化。

(4) Tolerance of violations of the company's code of conduct.

(4) 对于违反公司行为准则的容忍。

① Paragraph 9 of Auditing Standard No. 15, Audit Evidence.

审计准则第 15 号［审计证据］第 9 款。

② Denial of access to information might constitute a limitation on the scope of the audit that requires the auditor to qualify or disclaim an opinion. (See Auditing Standard No. 5, An Audit of Internal Control Over Financial Reporting That Is Integrated with An Audit of Financial Statements, and AU sec. 508, Reports on Audited Financial Statements.)

拒绝审计师接触资料可能构成审计范围限制，从而要求审计师发表有保留意见或否定意见（参见审计准则第 5 号［与财务报表审计合并执行的财务报告内部控制审计］和过渡审计准则第 508 条［报告经审计财务报表］）。

December 15, 2010

2010 年 12 月 15 日

AUDITING AND RELATED PROFESSIONAL PRACTICE STANDARDS

审计及相关专业实务准则

Auditing Standard No. 15 –

审计准则第 15 号 —

Audit Evidence

审计证据

PCAOB

Public Company Accounting Oversight Board

公众公司会计监管委员会

[Effective pursuant to SEC Release No. 34 – 63606, File No. PCAOB – 2010 – 01, December 23, 2010]

[按照 SEC 第 34 – 63606 号公告生效；文件号：PCAOB – 2010 – 01，2012 年 12 月 23 日]

Final Rule：PCAOB Release No. 2010 – 004

最终规则：PCAOB 公告第 2010 – 004 号

Table of Contents

目　　录

Paragraph

款　　号

Introduction
引　言

1. This standard explains what constitutes audit evidence and establishes requirements regarding designing and performing audit procedures to obtain sufficient appropriate audit evidence.

1. 本准则解释审计证据的构成，并为获取充分适当的审计证据所设计和实施审计程序制定要求。

2. Audit evidence is all the information, whether obtained from audit procedures or other sources, that is used by the auditor in arriving at the conclusions on which the auditor's opinion is based. Audit evidence consists of both information that supports and corroborates management's assertions regarding the financial statements or internal control over financial reporting and information that contradicts such assertions.

2. 审计证据是从审计程序或其他来源取得的被审计师用来得出结论的所有资料，而这些结论是审计师发表意见的基础。审计证据由两种组成，一种是支持和印证管理层有关财务报表或财务报告内部控制认定的资料，另一种是否定这些认定的资料。

Objective
目　标

3. The objective of the auditor is to plan and perform the audit to obtain appropriate audit evidence that is sufficient to support the opinion expressed in the auditor's report. ①

3. 审计师的目标是通过计划和实施审计程序获取足以支持其审计报告中所发表意见的适当的审计证据。

Sufficient Appropriate Audit Evidence
充分适当的审计证据

4. The auditor must plan and perform audit procedures to obtain sufficient appropriate audit evidence to provide a reasonable basis for his or her opinion.

4. 审计师必须计划和实施审计程序获取充分适当的审计为其发表审计意见提供合理的基础。

5. Sufficiency is the measure of the quantity of audit evidence. The quantity of audit evidence needed is affected by the following:

5. 充分性是审计证据数量的指标。所需审计证据的数量受到下列因素的影响：

- Risk of material misstatement (in the audit of financial statements) or the risk associated with the control (in the audit of internal control over financial reporting). As the risk increases, the amount of evidence that the auditor should obtain also increases. For example, ordinarily more evidence is needed to respond to significant risks. ②

- （财务报表审计中的）重大错报风险或（财务报告内部控制审计的）控制伴生的风险。随着风险增加，审计师应当获取的证据数量也增加。例如，为了应对重大风险，通常需要更多的证据。

- Quality of the audit evidence obtained. As the quality of the evidence increases , the need for additional corroborating evidence decreases. Obtaining more of the same type of audit evidence, however, cannot compensate for the poor quality of that evidence.

- 所获审计证据的质量。随着证据质量的提高，对于补充的印证性证据的需要降低。但是，获取更多相同类型的审计证据不能补偿该证据不良的质量。

6. Appropriateness is the measure of the quality of audit evidence, i. e. , its relevance

6. 适当性是审计证据的质量指标，比如，其相关

and reliability. To be appropriate, audit evidence must be both relevant and reliable in providing support for the conclusions on which the auditor's opinion is based.

性和可靠性。审计证据必须为审计意见所依据的结论提供相关和可靠的支持。

Relevance and Reliability
相关性和可靠性

7. Relevance. The relevance of audit evidence refers to its relationship to the assertion or to the objective of the control being tested. The relevance of audit evidence depends on:

7. 相关性。审计证据的相关性是指其与认定或受测控制的目标的关系。审计证据的相关性依赖于：

a. The design of the audit procedure used to test the assertion or control, in particular whether it is designed to (1) test the assertion or control directly and (2) test for understatement or overstatement; and

a. 用于测试认定或控制的审计程序的设计，尤其是它是否设计成（1）直接测试认定或控制和（2）测试低报或高报；和

b. The timing of the audit procedure used to test the assertion or control.

b. 用于测试认定或控制的审计程序的时间。

8. Reliability. The reliability of evidence depends on the nature and source of the evidence and the circumstances under which it is obtained. For example, in general:

8. 可靠性。证据的可靠性取决于证据的性质和来源，以及获取证据的具体情况。例如，一般来说：

• Evidence obtained from a knowledgeable source that is independent of the company is

• 从了解情况的独立来源获取的证据比仅从公司内

more reliable than evidence obtained only from internal company sources.

部获取的证据更可靠。

• The reliability of information generated internally by the company is increased when the company's controls over that information are effective.

• 当内部控制有效时，从公司内部生成的资料的可靠性就提高。

• Evidence obtained directly by the auditor is more reliable than evidence obtained indirectly.

• 审计师直接获取的证据比间接获取的证据可靠。

• Evidence provided by original documents is more reliable than evidence provided by photocopies or facsimiles, or documents that have been filmed, digitized, or otherwise converted into electronic form, the reliability of which depends on the controls over the conversion and maintenance of those documents.

• 原始资料提供的证据比复印件或传真件、拍摄的、电子化的、甚至是转换成电子形式的文档提供的证据更可靠，这些证据的可靠性有赖于对转换和维护这些文档的控制。

9. The auditor is not expected to be an expert in document authentication. However, if conditions indicate that a document may not be authentic or that the terms in a document have been modified but that the modifications have not been disclosed to the auditor, the auditor should modify the planned audit procedures or perform additional audit procedures to respond to those conditions and

9. 审计师不被要求成为文档鉴定的专家。但是，如果情况表明某个文档可能不是真实的，或者某个文档中的条款已被修改，而该修改没有向审计师披露，审计师应当修改预定审计程序或实施补充审计程序，应对这些情况，并

should evaluate the effect, if any, on the other aspects of the audit.

且，如果有的话，应当评价其对于审计其他方面的影响。

Using Information Produced by the Company

利用公司提供的资料

10. When using information produced by the company as audit evidence, the auditor should evaluate whether the information is sufficient and appropriate for purposes of the audit by performing procedures to: ③

10. 当利用公司提供的资料作为审计证据时，审计师应当通过实施以下程序，评价该资料对于本审计是否充分和适当：

- Test the accuracy and completeness of the information, or test the controls over the accuracy and completeness of that information; and

- 测试该资料的准确性和完整性，或者，测试其准确性和完整性控制；和

- Evaluate whether the information is sufficiently precise and detailed for purposes of the audit.

- 评价该资料对于本审计而言是否充分地精确和详尽。

Financial Statement Assertions

财务报表认定

11. In representing that the financial statements are presented fairly in conformity with the applicable financial reporting framework, management implicitly or explicitly makes as-

11. 当管理层表示财务报表遵循适当的财务报告框架公允列报时，对财务报表和相关披露的诸多要素

sertions regarding the recognition, measurement, presentation, and disclosure of the various elements of financial statements and related disclosures. Those assertions can be classified into the following categories:

的确认、计量、列报和披露做出了隐含或明确的认定。这些认定可以分为下列类型：

• *Existence or occurrence* – Assets or liabilities of the company exist at a given date, and recorded transactions have occurred during a given period.

• *存在或发生：* 公司的资产或负债在给定日期存在，并且，账载交易在给定期间已经发生。

• *Completeness* – All transactions and accounts that should be presented in the financial statements are so included.

• *完整性：* 所有应当被列报在财务报表中的交易和账户都被包括在内。

• *Valuation or allocation* – Asset, liability, equity, revenue, and expense components have been included in the financial statements at appropriate amounts.

• *估价或分摊：* 资产、负债、权益、收入和费用等组成部分已被以适当的金额包括在财务报表中。

• *Rights and obligations* – The company holds or controls rights to the assets, and liabilities are obligations of the company at a given date.

• *权利和义务：* 在给定日期，公司拥有或控制对资产的权利，并且，对负债承担义务。

• *Presentation and disclosure* – The components of the financial statements are properly classified, described, and disclosed.

• *列报和披露：* 财务报表的组成部分被适当地分类、描述和披露。

12. The auditor may base his or her work on

12. 审计师可以将其工作

financial statement assertions that differ from those in this standard if the assertions are sufficient for the auditor to identify the types of potential misstatements and to respond appropriately to the risks of material misstatement in each significant account and disclosure that has a reasonable possibility④ of containing misstatements that would cause the financial statements to be materially misstated, individually or in combination with other misstatements. ⑤

基于不同于本准则的财务报表认定，只要这些认定足以使审计师识别潜在错报风险的类型，适当地应对每个重要账户和披露中的重大错报风险，它们有合理的可能性包含了错报，这些错报，单独或与连同其他错报一起，可能导致财务报表重大错报。

Audit Procedures for Obtaining Audit Evidence

获取审计证据的审计程序

13. Audit procedures can be classified into the following categories:

13. 审计程序可以分为以下几类：

a. Risk assessment procedures, ⑥ and

b. Further audit procedures, ⑦ which consist of:

a. 风险评估程序，和

b. 进一步审计程序，包括：

(1) Tests of controls, and

(1) 控制测试，和

(2) Substantive procedures, including tests of details and? substantive analytical procedures.

(2) 实质性程序，包括细节测试和实质性分析程序。

14. Paragraphs 15 – 21 of this standard describe specific audit procedures. The purpose

14. 本准则第 15 至 21 款描述特别审计程序。某个

of an audit procedure determines whether it is a risk assessment procedure, test of controls, or substantive procedure.

审计程序的目的决定它是一个风险评估程序、控制测试还是实质性程序。

Inspection

检查

15. Inspection involves examining records or documents, whether internal or external, in paper form, electronic form, or other media, or physically examining an asset. Inspection of records and documents provides audit evidence of varying degrees of reliability, depending on their nature and source and, in the case of internal records and documents, on the effectiveness of the controls over their production. An example of inspection used as a test of controls is inspection of records for evidence of authorization.

15. 检查涉及检查内部或外部的书面形式、电子形式或其他介质的记录或文档，或者实地检查某个资产。记录和文档的检查可以提供可靠程度不同的审计证据，审计证据的可靠性有赖于其性质和来源；对于内部记录和文档，还有赖于生成它们的控制的有效性。用作控制测试的检查一个例子是为了审批证据而检查记录。

Observation

观察

16. Observation consists of looking at a process or procedure being performed by others, e. g. , the auditor's observation of inventory counting by the company's personnel or the performance of control activities. Observation can provide audit evidence about the performance of a process or procedure, but the evidence is limit-

16. 观察由查看正在由他人执行的某个过程或流程，比如，审计师观察公司员工执行的盘点或实施的控制活动。观察可以提供某个过程或流程执行的审计证据，但是，该证据

ed to the point in time at which the observation takes place and also is limited by the fact that the act of being observed may affect how the process or procedure is performed. ⑧

局限于观察所发生的时点，而且还受限于被观察的该动作可能影响该过程或流程如何被执行。

Inquiry
询问

17. Inquiry consists of seeking information from knowledgeable persons in financial or nonfinancial roles within the company or outside the company. Inquiry may be performed throughout the audit in addition to other audit procedures. Inquiries may range from formal written inquiries to informal oral inquiries. Evaluating responses to inquiries is an integral part of the inquiry process. ⑨

17. 询问包括向熟悉情况的公司内部担任财务或非财务角色的人员或外部人员寻找资料。询问可以可以作为其他审计程序的补充在审计的全过程实施。询问可以是正式的书面询问或非正式的口头询问。评价询问的回复是询问过程不可分割的一部分。

Note: Inquiry of company personnel, by itself, does not provide sufficient audit evidence to reduce audit risk to an appropriately low level for a relevant assertion or to support a conclusion about the effectiveness of a control.

注：询问公司员工本身不能提供充分的审计证据将某个相关认定的审计风险降低到适当的低水平，或者，支持关于控制有效性的结论。

Confirmation
函证

18. A confirmation response represents a par-

18. 函证回函代表审计师

ticular form of audit evidence obtained by the auditor from a third party in accordance with PCAOB standards. ⑩

遵照 PCAOB 准则从第三方获取审计证据的一种特定形式。

Recalculation
重新计算

19. Recalculation consists of checking the mathematical accuracy of documents or records. Recalculation may be performed manually or electronically.

19. 重新计算包括核对文档或记录的算术准确性。重新计算可以人工方式或电子方式实施。

Reperformance
重新执行

20. Reperformance involves the independent execution of procedures or controls that were originally performed by company personnel.

20. 重新执行涉及独立执行最初由公司员工执行的流程或控制。

Analytical Procedures
分析性程序

21. Analytical procedures consist of evaluations of financial information made by a study of plausible relationships among both financial and nonfinancial data. Analytical procedures also encompass the investigation of significant differences from expected amounts. ⑪

21. 分析性程序包括以研究财务和非财务数据之间的合理关系来评价财务资料。分析性程序也包括调查与预期金额的重大差异。

Selecting Items for Testing to Obtain Audit Evidence
为获取审计证据选择测试项目

22. Designing substantive tests of details and tests of controls includes determining the means of selecting items for testing from among the items included in an account or the occurrences of a control. The auditor should determine the means of selecting items for testing to obtain evidence that, in combination with other relevant evidence, is sufficient to meet the objective of the audit procedure. The alternative means of selecting items for testing are:

- Selecting all items;
- Selecting specific items; and
- Audit sampling.

22. 设计实质性细节测试和控制测试包括确定从账户项目或控制事件中选择测试项目的方法。审计师应当为测试确定选择项目的方法，获取的证据与其他相关证据一起，足以满足审计程序的目标。可以用于为测试选择项目的方法是:

- 选择所有项目;
- 选择特定项目; 和
- 审计抽样

23. The particular means or combination of means of selecting items for testing that is appropriate depends on the nature of the audit procedure, the characteristics of the control or the items in the account being tested, and the evidence necessary to meet the objective of the audit procedure.

23. 适当地为测试选择项目特定方法或方法的组合取决于审计程序的性质、控制或受测账户的项目以及满足审计程序目标所需证据的特点。

Selecting All Items
选择所有项目

24. Selecting all items (100 percent examination) refers to testing the entire population of items in an account or the entire population of occurrences of a control (or an entire stratum within one of those populations). The following are examples of situations in which 100 percent examination might be applied:

24. 选择所有项目（百分之百检查）是指测试账户项目的整个样本总体或控制事件的整个样本总体（或者这些样本总体中的某个整个分层）。以下是运用百分之百检查的情况举例：

- The population constitutes a small number of large value items;

- 样本总体由少量的大额项目组成；

- The audit procedure is designed to respond to a significant risk, and other means of selecting items for testing do not provide sufficient appropriate audit evidence; and

- 审计程序被设计成应对重大风险，并且，其他选择测试项目的方法不能提供充分适当的审计证据；和

- The audit procedure can be automated effectively and applied to the entire population.

- 审计程序可以被有效地自动化，并且被运用于整个样本总体。

Selecting Specific Items
选择特定项目

25. Selecting specific items refers to testing all of the items in a population that have a specified characteristic, such as:

25. 选择特定项目是指测试某个具有特定属性的样本总体的全部项目，比如：

• Key items. The auditor may decide to select specific items within a population because they are important to accomplishing the objective of the audit procedure or exhibit some other characteristic, e. g. , items that are suspicious, unusual, or particularly risk -prone or items that have a history of error.

• 关键项目：审计师可以决定选择某个样本总体的特定项目，由于它们对于达成审计程序的目标或展现某些其他特点是重要的，比如，可疑的、不寻常的或者有特定风险倾向的项目，或者曾经出错的项目。

• All items over a certain amount. The auditor may decide to examine items whose recorded values exceed a certain amount to verify a large proportion of the total amount of the items included in an account.

• 大于特定金额的所有项目：审计师可以决定检查账载价值超过特定金额的项目，检验账户包含的项目总金额的大部分。

26. The auditor also might select specific items to obtain an understanding about matters such as the nature of the company or the nature of transactions.

26. 审计师也可以选择特定项目用于了解公司性质及其交易性质等问题。

27. The application of audit procedures to items that are selected as described in paragraphs 25 –26 of this standard does not constitute audit sampling, and the results of those audit procedures cannot be projected to the entire population. ⑫

27. 对遵照本准则第 25 至 26 款的描述选择的项目实施审计程序不构成审计抽样，而且，这些审计程序的结果不能用于推断整个样本总体。

Audit Sampling
审计抽样

28. Audit sampling is the application of an au-

28. 审计抽样是为了评价

dit procedure to less than 100 percent of the items within an account balance or class of transactions for the purpose of evaluating some characteristic of the balance or class. [13]

账户余额或交易类型的某些特点而对其中少于百分之百的项目运用审计程序。

Inconsistency in, or Doubts about the Reliability of, Audit Evidence
审计证据的不一致性或对其可靠性的怀疑

29. If audit evidence obtained from one source is inconsistent with that obtained from another, or if the auditor has doubts about the reliability of information to be used as audit evidence, the auditor should perform the audit procedures necessary to resolve the matter and should determine the effect, if any, on other aspects of the audit.

29. 如果某个来源获取的审计证据与另一个来源的证据不一致，或者，审计师怀疑将要被用作审计证据的资料的可靠性，审计师应当实施必要的审计程序解决该问题，并且，如果有的话，应当确定其对于审计的其他方面的影响。

---

① Auditing Standard No. 14, Evaluating Audit Results, establishes requirements regarding evaluating whether sufficient appropriate evidence has been obtained. Auditing Standard No. 3, Audit Documentation, establishes requirements regarding documenting the procedures performed, evidence obtained, and conclusions reached in an audit.

审计准则第 14 号［评价审计结果］为评价是否已获取充分适当的证据制定要求。审计准则第 3 号［审计文档］为归档被实施程序、获取的证据和审计结论制定要求。

② Paragraph A5 of Auditing Standard No. 12, Identifying and Assessing Risks of Material Misstatement.

审计准则第 12 号［识别和评估重大错报风险］第 A5 款。

③ When using the work of a specialist engaged or employed by management, see AU sec. 336, Using the Work of a Specialist. When using information produced by a service organization or a service auditor's report as audit evidence, see AU sec. 324, Service Organizations, and for integrated audits, see Auditing Standard No. 5, An Audit of Internal Control Over Financial Reporting That Is Integrated with An Audit of Financial Statements.

当利用管理层聘用或雇用的专家的工作时，参见过渡审计准则第 336 条［利用专家的工作］。当利用服务组织或服务审计师的报告生成的资料作为审计证据时，参见过渡审计准则第 324 条［服务组织］，对于整合审计，参见审计准则第 5 号［与财务报表审计合并执行的财务报告内部控制审计］。

④ There is a reasonable possibility of an event, as used in this standard, when the likelihood of the event is either "reasonably possible" or "probable," as those terms are used in the FASB Accounting Standards Codification, Contingencies Topic, paragraph 450 – 20 – 25 – 1.

本准则所称某事件存在合理的可能性是指该事件的发生要么“合理的可能”，要么“有可能”，这两个词汇的定义与美国财务会计准则委员会“会计准则汇编”［或有事项］第 450 – 20 – 25 – 1 款的定义一致。

⑤ For an integrated audit, also see paragraph 28 of Auditing Standard No. 5.

对于整合审计，参见审计准则第 5 号第 28 款。

⑥ Auditing Standard No. 12.

审计准则第 12 号。

⑦ Auditing Standard No. 13, The auditor's Responses to the Risks of Material Misstatement.

审计准则第 13 号［审计师对于重大错报风险的应对策略］。

⑧ AU sec. 331, Inventories, establishes requirements regarding observation of the counting of inventory.

过渡审计准则第 331 条［存货］为存货监盘制定要求。

⑨ AU sec. 333, Management Representations, establishes requirements regarding written management representations, including confirmation of management responses to oral inquiries.

过渡审计准则第 333 号［管理层声明］为书面管理层声明，包括管理层对于书面询问答复的确认，制定要求。

⑩ AU sec. 330, The Confirmation Process.

过渡审计准则第 330 号［函证］。

⑪ AU sec. 329, Substantive Analytical Procedures, establishes requirements on performing analytical procedures as substantive procedures.

过渡审计准则第 329 条［实质性分析程序］为作为实质性程序而实施分析性程序制定要求。

⑫ If misstatements are identified in the selected items, see paragraphs 12 – 13 and paragraphs 17 – 19 of Auditing Standard No. 14.

如果在选择的项目中发现错报，参见审计准则第 14 号第 12 至 13 款和 17 至 19 款。

⑬ AU sec. 350, Audit Sampling, establishes requirements regarding audit sampling.

过渡审计准则第 350 条［审计抽样］为审计抽样制定要求。

December 15, 2010
2010 年 12 月 15 日

AUDITING AND RELATED PROFESSIONAL PRACTICE STANDARDS
审计及相关专业实务准则

Auditing Standard No. 16 –
审计准则第 16 号 —

Communications with Audit Committees
与审计委员会沟通

PCAOB

Public Company Accounting Oversight Board
公众公司会计监管委员会

[Effective pursuant to SEC Release No. 34 – 63606, File No. PCAOB – 2010 – 01, December 23, 2010]
[按照 SEC 第 34 – 63606 号公告生效；文件号：PCAOB – 2010 – 01，2012 年 12 月 23 日]

Final Rule：PCAOB Release No. 2010 – 004
最终规则：PCAOB 公告第 2010 – 004 号

Table of Contents

目　　录

Paragraph
款　　号

Introduction

引　　言

1. This standard requires the auditor to communicate with the company's audit committee① regarding certain matters related to the conduct of an audit② and to obtain certain information from the audit committee relevant to the audit. This standard also requires the auditor to establish an understanding of the terms of the audit engagement with the audit committee and to record that understanding in an engagement letter.

1. 本准则要求审计师就审计执行的有关事项与公司的审计委员会沟通，并从审计委员会取得与审计有关的某些资料。本准则还要求审计师与审计委员会就审计业务约定书的条款达成谅解，并在业务约定书中记载该谅解。

2. Other Public Company Accounting Oversight Board ("PCAOB") rules and standards identify additional matters to be communicated to a company's audit committee (see Appendix B). Various laws or regulations also require the auditor to communicate certain matters to the audit committee. ③ The communication requirements of this standard do not modify or replace communications to the audit committee required by such other PCAOB rules and standards, and other laws or regulations. Nothing in this standard precludes the auditor from communicating other matters to the audit committee.

2. 公众公司会计监督委员会（"PCAOB"）的其他规则和准则指出需要向公司审计委员会通报的补充事项（参见附录 B）。各种法律或法规还要求审计师向审计委员会通报某些事项。本准则的通报要求不改变或代替那些 PCAOB 规则和准则以及其他法律或法规要求的向审计委员会的通报。本准则不禁止审计师向审计委员会通报其他事项。

Objective
目　标

3. The objectives of the auditor are to:

3. 审计师的目标是：

a. Communicate to the audit committee the responsibilities of the auditor in relation to the audit and establish an understanding of the terms of the audit engagement with the audit committee;

a. 向审计委员会通报审计师在审计中的责任，并与审计委员会就审计业务达成谅解；

b. Obtain information from the audit committee relevant to the audit;

b. 从审计委员会获得审计有关的资料；

c. Communicate to the audit committee an overview of the overall audit strategy and timing of the audit; and

c. 向审计委员会通报总体审计战略和审计时间的概略情况；

d. Provide the audit committee with timely observations arising from the audit that are significant to the financial reporting process.

d. 及时向审计委员会提供对于财务报告过程重大的审计发现。

Note: "Communicate to," as used in this standard, is meant to encourage effective two - way communication between the auditor and the audit committee throughout the audit to assist in understanding matters relevant to the audit.

注：本准则所说"通报"是为了鼓励审计师与审计委员会之间贯穿审计过程的有效的双向交流，帮助了解与审计有关的问题。

Appointment and Retention
任命和留用

Significant Issues Discussed with Management in Connection with the auditor's Appointment or Retention
与管理层讨论关于审计师任命或留用的重大事项

4. The auditor should discuss with the audit committee any significant issues that the auditor discussed with management in connection with the appointment or retention of the auditor, including significant discussions regarding the application of accounting principles and auditing standards.

4. 审计师应当与审计委员会讨论审计师与管理层讨论的与审计师的任命或留用有关的任何重大事项，包括与会计政策和审计准则的运用有关的重大讨论。

Establish an Understanding of the Terms of the Audit
达成审计条款的谅解

5. The auditor should establish an understanding of the terms of the audit engagement with the audit committee. This understanding includes communicating to the audit committee the following:

5. 审计师应当与审计委员会达成审计业务条款的谅解。该谅解包括向审计委员会沟通以下事项：

a. The objective of the audit;

a. 审计的目标；

b. The responsibilities of the auditor; and

b. 审计师的责任；和

c. The responsibilities of management.

c. 管理层的责任。

6. The auditor should record the understand-

6. 审计师应当在业务约

ing of the terms of the audit engagement in an engagement letter and provide the engagement letter to the audit committee annually. The auditor should have the engagement letter executed by the appropriate party or parties on behalf of the company. ④ If the appropriate party or parties are other than the audit committee, or its chair on behalf of the audit committee, the auditor should determine that the audit committee has acknowledged and agreed to the terms of the engagement.

定书中记载审计业务条款的谅解，并每年向审计委员会提交该业务约定书。审计师应当要求代表公司的适当对象履行该业务约定书。如果审计委员会或代行其职权的主席不是适当对象，审计师应当确定审计委员会已经知悉并同意业务条款。

Note: Appendix C describes matters that the auditor should include in the engagement letter about the terms of the audit engagement.

注：附录 C 描述审计师应当包括在业务约定书中的审计业务条款。

7. If the auditor cannot establish an understanding of the terms of the audit engagement with the audit committee, the auditor should decline to accept, continue, or perform the engagement.

7. 如果审计师不能与审计委员会就审计业务条款达成谅解，审计师应当拒绝接受、继续或执行该业务。

Obtaining Information and Communicating the Audit Strategy

获取资料和通报审计策略

Obtaining Information Relevant to the Audit

取得与审计相关的资料

8. The auditor should inquire of the audit

8. 审计师应当询问审计

committee about whether it is aware of matters relevant to the audit, ⑤ including, but not limited to, violations or possible violations of laws or regulations. ⑥

委员会是否知悉审计有关事项，包括但不限于，触犯或可能触犯法律或法规的情况。

Overall Audit Strategy, Timing of the Audit, and Significant Risks

总体审计策略、审计时间和重大风险

9. The auditor should communicate to the audit committee an overview of the overall audit strategy, including the timing of the audit, ⑦ and discuss with the audit committee the significant risks identified during the auditor's risk assessment procedures. ⑧

9. 审计师应当向审计委员会概要地通报总体审计策略，包括审计的时间，并与审计委员会讨论审计师风险评估程序识别的重大风险。

Note: This overview is intended to provide information about the audit, but not specific details that would compromise the effectiveness of the audit procedures.

注：该概要是用于提供关于审计的信息，但不包括具体细节，通报审计具体细节会损害审计程序的有效性。

10. As part of communicating the overall audit strategy, the auditor should communicate the following matters to the audit committee, if applicable:

10. 作为沟通总体审计策略的一部分，如果适当的话，审计师应当与审计委员会沟通下列事项：

a. The nature and extent of specialized skill or knowledge needed to perform the planned audit procedures or evaluate the audit results

a. 实施预定审计程序或评价与重大风险有关的审计结果所需的特殊技能或

related to significant risks; [9]

知识的性质和范围；

b. The extent to which the auditor plans to use the work of the company's internal auditors in an audit of financial statements; [10]

b. 审计师计划在财务报表审计中利用公司内部审计师工作的范围；

c. The extent to which the auditor plans to use the work of internal auditors, company personnel (in addition to internal auditors), and third parties working under the direction of management or the audit committee when performing an audit of internal control over financial reporting; [11]

c. 审计师计划在实施财务报告内部控制审计时，利用内部审计师、（内部审计师之外的）公司员工和接受管理层或审计委员会指导的第三方工作的范围；

d. The names, locations, and planned responsibilities [12] of other independent public accounting firms or other persons, who are not employed by the auditor, that perform audit procedures in the current period audit; and

Note: The term "other independent public accounting firms" in the context of this communication includes firms that perform audit procedures in the current period audit regardless of whether they otherwise have any relationship with the auditor.

d. 在本期审计中实施审计程序的不是由本审计师雇佣的其他独立会计师事务所或人员的名称、地址和预定责任；和

注：本沟通所说的"其他独立会计师事务所"包括在本期审计中实施审计程序的事务所，而不论其是否与本审计师有任何关系。

e. The basis for the auditor's determination that the auditor can serve as principal auditor, if significant parts of the audit are to be performed by other auditors. [13]

e. 如果该审计的重大部分将由其他审计师实施，审计师确定本人可以担任主责审计师的依据。

11. The auditor should communicate to the audit committee significant changes to the planned audit strategy or the significant risks initially identified and the reasons for such changes. ⑭

11. 审计师应当向审计委员会通报预定审计策略或者初始识别的重大风险的重大变化，以及这些变化的理由。

Results of the Audit

审计结果

Accounting Policies and Practices, Estimates, and Significant Unusual Transactions

会计政策和实务、估计和重大异常交易

12. The auditor should communicate to the audit committee the following matters:

12. 审计师应当向审计委员会通报下列事项：

a. Significant accounting policies and practices. ⑮

a. 重大会计政策和实务。

(1) Management's initial selection of, or changes in, significant accounting policies or the application of such policies in the current period; and

(1) 管理层对于重大会计政策的初始选择或变更，或者，这些政策在本期的运用；和

(2) The effect on financial statements or disclosures of significant accounting policies in (i) controversial areas or (ii) areas for which there is a lack of authoritative guidance or consensus, or diversity in practice.

(2) 重大会计政策在（1）有争议领域或（2）缺乏权威性指引或一致意见以及实务多样化的领域对于财务报表或披露的影响。

b. Critical accounting policies and practices. All critical accounting policies and practices to be used, including: ⑯

b. 关键会计政策和实务。采用的所有关键会计政策和实务，包括：

(1) The reasons certain policies and practices are considered critical; and

（1）某些政策和实务被认为是关键的理由；和

(2) How current and anticipated future events might affect the determination of whether certain policies and practices are considered critical.

（2）当期事件和预期的未来事件会如何影响对于某些政策和实务是否被认为是关键的决定。

Note: Critical accounting policies and practices, as defined in Appendix A, are a company's accounting policies and practices that are both most important to the portrayal of the company's financial condition and results, and require management's most difficult, subjective, or complex judgments, often as a result of the need to make estimates about the effects of matters that are inherently uncertain. Critical accounting policies and practices are tailored to specific events in the current year, and the accounting policies and practices that are considered critical might change from year to year.

注：附录 A 定义的关键会计政策和实务是对于描绘公司的财务状况和成果最重要的会计政策和实务，并且，需要管理层做出最困难、主观或复杂的判断，通常是由于需要对固有不确定性的事项的影响做出估计。关键会计政策和实务是为当年的具体事件量身订制的，并且，这些被认为是关键的会计政策和实务可能逐年变化。

c. Critical accounting estimates.

c. 关键会计估计

(1) A description of the process manage-

（1）对于管理层用于形

ment used to develop critical accounting estimates; [17]

成关键会计估计的流程的描述；

(2) Management's significant assumptions used in critical accounting estimates that have a high degree of subjectivity; [18] and

（2）管理层用于关键会计估计的具有很高程度主观性的重大假设；和

(3) Any significant changes management made to the processes used to develop critical accounting estimates or significant assumptions, a description of management's reasons for the changes, and the effects of the changes on the financial statements. [19]

（3）管理层对于用来形成关键会计估计或重大假设流程的任何重大变化，管理层对于这些变化的理由的描述，以及这些变化对于财务报表的影响。

d. Significant unusual transactions.

d. 重大不寻常交易。

(1) Significant transactions that are outside the normal course of business for the company or that otherwise appear to be unusual due to their timing, size, or nature; [20] and

（1）公司日常业务过程之外的重大交易，或者，从时间、大小或性质上看起来不寻常的交易；和

(2) The policies and practices management used to account for significant unusual transactions.

（2）管理层用于核算重大不寻常交易的政策和实务。

Note: As part of its communications to the audit committee, management might communicate some or all of the matters in paragraph 12. If management communicates any of these matters, the auditor does not need to communicate them at the same level of detail as

注：作为与审计委员会沟通的一部分，管理层可以沟通第 12 款的某些或全部事项。如果管理层沟通了任何上述事项，审计师不必再以同样详细的程度

management, as long as the auditor (1) participated in management's discussion with the audit committee, (2) affirmatively confirmed to the audit committee that management has adequately communicated these matters, and (3) with respect to critical accounting policies and practices, identified for the audit committee those accounting policies and practices that the auditor considers critical. The auditor should communicate any omitted or inadequately described matters to the audit committee.

沟通，只要审计师（1）参与了管理层与审计委员会的沟通，（2）向审计委员会正面确认管理层已经充分沟通这些事项，并且（3）对于关键会计政策和实务，为审计委员会识别了审计师认为关键的那些会计政策和实务。

Auditor's Evaluation of the Quality of the Company's Financial Reporting

审计师对于公司财务报告质量的评价

13. The auditor should communicate to the audit committee the following matters:

13. 审计师应当向审计委员会通报下列事项：

a. Qualitative aspects of significant accounting policies and practices.

a. 重大会计政策和实务的质量方面。

(1) The results of the auditor's evaluation of, and conclusions about, the qualitative aspects of the company's significant accounting policies and practices, including situations in which the auditor identified bias in management's judgments about the amounts and disclosures in the financial statements; [21] and

（1）审计师关于公司重大会计政策和实务的质量方面的评价结果，包括审计师识别的管理层对于财务报表金额和披露的判断中的偏好等情况；和

(2) The results of the auditor's evaluation of the differences between (i) estimates best supported by the audit evidence and (ii) estimates included in the financial statements, which are individually reasonable, that indicate a possible bias on the part of the company's management. ㉒

(2)审计师对于(1)审计证据支持的最佳估计与(2)包括在财务报表中的个别合理的估计之间的差额的评价，该差额表明公司管理层方面某种可能的偏好。

b. Assessment of critical accounting policies and practices. The auditor's assessment of management's disclosures related to the critical accounting policies and practices, along with any significant modifications to the disclosure of those policies and practices proposed by the auditor that management did not make.

b. 关键会计政策和实务的评估。审计师对于管理层有关关键会计政策和实务的评估，以及管理层拒绝审计师提出的对于这些政策和实务披露的任何重大修改情况。

c. Conclusions regarding critical accounting estimates. The basis for the auditor's conclusions regarding the reasonableness of the critical accounting estimates. ㉓

c. 关于重大会计估计的结论。审计师关于关键会计估计合理性的结论的依据。

d. Significant unusual transactions. The auditor's understanding of the business rationale for significant unusual transactions. ㉔

d. 重大不寻常交易。审计师对于重大非寻常交易的商业理念的理解。

e. Financial statement presentation. The results of the auditor's evaluation of whether

e. 财务报表列报。审计师对于财务报表及其相关

the presentation of the financial statements and the related disclosures are in conformity with the applicable financial reporting framework, including the auditor's consideration of the form, arrangement, and content of the financial statements (including the accompanying notes), encompassing matters such as the terminology used, the amount of detail given, the classification of items, and the bases of amounts set forth. ㉕

披露的列报是否遵循适当的财务报告框架的评价结果，包括审计师对于财务报表的形式、安排和内容的考虑（包括报表附注），涵盖诸如术语的运用、显示细节的数量、报表项目的分类和上述金额的列报基础等事项。

f. New accounting pronouncements. Situations in which, as a result of the auditor's procedures, the auditor identified a concern regarding management's anticipated application of accounting pronouncements that have been issued but are not yet effective and might have a significant effect on future financial reporting.

f. 新的会计公告。作为审计程序的结果，审计师识别的关于管理层对于已发布但未生效的对于未来财务报告有重大影响的会计公告的预期运用的关切。

g. Alternative accounting treatments. All alternative treatments permissible under the applicable financial reporting framework for policies and practices related to material items that have been discussed with management, including the ramifications of the use of such alternative disclosures and treatments and the treatment preferred by the auditor. ㉖

g. 可选会计处理。对于已经与管理层讨论的与重大项目的政策和实务有关的适当的会计报告框架允许的所有可选会计处理，包括运用这些可选披露和处理的后果以及审计师优先选择的处理方式。

Other Information in Documents Containing Audited Financial Statements
包含在经审计财务报表文件中的其他资料

14. When other information is presented in documents containing audited financial statements, the auditor should communicate to the audit committee the auditor's responsibility under PCAOB rules and standards for such information, any related procedures performed, and the results of such procedures. [27]

14. 当其他资料被列报在包含经审计财务报表的文件中时，审计师应当向审计委员会通报审计师根据 PCAOB 规则和准则对于这些资料的责任、实施的相关程序和这些程序的结果。

Difficult or Contentious Matters for which the Auditor Consulted
审计师咨询难题或争议事项

15. The auditor should communicate to the audit committee matters that are difficult or contentious for which the auditor consulted outside the engagement team and that the auditor reasonably determined are relevant to the audit committee's oversight of the financial reporting process.

15. 审计师应当向审计委员会通报审计师在业务团队之外咨询难题或争议事项，以及审计师合理地确定与审计委员会财务报告过程监管有关的事项。

Management Consultation with Other Accountants
管理层向其他会计师咨询

16. When the auditor is aware that manage-

16. 当审计师知悉管理层

ment consulted with other accountants about significant auditing or accounting matters and the auditor has identified a concern regarding such matters, the auditor should communicate to the audit committee his or her views about such matters that were the subject of such consultation.

向其他会计师咨询有关重大审计或会计事项，而且，审计师已经识别了这些事项，审计师应当向审计委员会通报对于这些咨询事项的看法。

Going Concern
持续经营

17. The auditor should communicate to the audit committee, when applicable, the following matters relating to the auditor's evaluation of the company's ability to continue as a going concern: ㉘

17. 如果适当，审计师应当向审计委员会通报下列与审计师对于公司的持续经营能力的评价有关的事项：

a. If the auditor believes there is substantial doubt about the company's ability to continue as a going concern for a reasonable period of time, the conditions and events that the auditor identified that, when considered in the aggregate, indicate that there is substantial doubt; ㉙

a. 审计师识别的如果合并考虑则暗示该能力存在严重疑问的状况和事件（如果审计师相信公司在合理时期内持续经营能力存在严重疑问）；

b. If the auditor concludes, after consideration of management's plans, that substantial doubt about the company's ability to continue as a going concern is alleviated, the basis for the auditor's conclusion, including elements the

b. 如果审计师在考虑了管理层的计划之后认为对于公司持续经营能力的严重疑问已被缓解，审计师得出上述结论的依据，包

auditor identified within management's plans that are significant to overcoming the adverse effects of the conditions and events; [30]

括审计师在管理层计划中识别的对于战胜这些状况或事件的负面影响而言重大的要素；

c. If the auditor concludes, after consideration of management's plans, that substantial doubt about the company's ability to continue as a going concern for a reasonable period of time remains: [31]

c. 如果审计师在考虑了管理层的计划之后认为对于公司持续经营能力的严重疑问仍然存在：

(1) The effects, if any, on the financial statements and the adequacy of the related disclosure; [32] and

(1) 对于财务报表和相关披露充分性的影响，如果有的话；和

(2) The effects on the auditor's report. [33]

(2) 对于审计报告的影响。

Uncorrected and Corrected Misstatements
未纠正和已纠正的错报

18. The auditor should provide the audit committee with the schedule of uncorrected misstatements related to accounts and disclosures[34] that the auditor presented to management. [35] The auditor should discuss with the audit committee, or determine that management has adequately discussed with the audit committee, the basis for the determination that the uncorrected misstatements were im-

18. 审计师应当向审计委员会提交审计师提供给管理层的与账户或披露有关的未纠正错报表。审计师应当与审计委员会讨论或者确定管理层已经与审计委员会充分讨论，决定这些未纠正错报不重大的依据，包括考虑到的质量因素。审计师还应当通报未

material, including the qualitative factors[36] considered. The auditor also should communicate that uncorrected misstatements or matters underlying those uncorrected misstatements could potentially cause future – period financial statements to be materially misstated, even if the auditor has concluded that the uncorrected misstatements are immaterial to the financial statements under audit.

纠正错报或导致这些未纠正错报的事项可能潜在地造成未来期间财务报表被重大错报，尽管审计师已经认定这些未纠正错报对于本次审计的财务报表不重大。

19. The auditor should communicate to the audit committee those corrected misstatements, other than those that are clearly trivial, [37] related to accounts and disclosures that might not have been detected except through the auditing procedures performed, and discuss with the audit committee the implications that such corrected misstatements might have on the company's financial reporting process.

19. 审计师应当向审计委员会通报明显的小差错之外的那些与账户和披露有关的已纠正错报，除非通过实施审计程序，否则这些错报也许不会被发现，并与审计委员会讨论这些已纠正错报对于公司财务报告过程的寓意。

Material Written Communications
重要书面沟通

20. The auditor should communicate to the audit committee other material written communications between the auditor and management. [38]

20. 审计师应当向审计委员会通报审计师与管理层之间的其他重要沟通。

Departure from the auditor's Standard Report
非标准审计报告

21. The auditor should communicate to the audit committee the following matters related to the auditor's report:

21. 审计师应当向审计委员会通报与审计报告有关的下列事项：

a. When the auditor expects to modify the opinion in the auditor's report, the reasons for the modification, and the wording of the report; and

a. 当审计师预期修改审计报告的意见时，修改的理由和报告的措辞；和

b. When the auditor expects to include explanatory language or an explanatory paragraph in the auditor's report, the reasons for the explanatory language or paragraph, and the wording of the explanatory language or paragraph.

b. 当审计师预期在审计报告中包括说明性用语或说明段时，使用说明性用语或说明段的理由及其措辞。

Disagreements with Management
与管理层意见相左

22. The auditor should communicate to the audit committee any disagreements with management about matters, whether or not satisfactorily resolved, that individually or in the aggregate could be significant to the company's financial statements or the auditor's report. Disagreements with management do not include differences of opinion based on in-

22. 审计师应当向审计委员会通报与管理层那些单独或合并的对于财务报表或审计报告而言可能重大的事项的任何不同意见，无论是否满意解决。与管理层的不同意见不包括那些随后由审计师在发布审

complete facts or preliminary information that are later resolved by the auditor obtaining additional relevant facts or information prior to the issuance of the auditor's report.

计报告之前取得进一步的相关事实或资料而解决的基于不完整事实或初步资料的意见分歧。

Difficulties Encountered in Performing the Audit
在实施审计中遭遇的困难

23. The auditor should communicate to the audit committee any significant difficulties encountered during the audit. Significant difficulties encountered during the audit include, but are not limited to:

23. 审计师应当向审计委员会通报在审计中遭遇的任何重大困难。在审计中遭遇的任何重大困难包括，但不限于：

a. Significant delays by management, the unavailability of company personnel, or an unwillingness by management to provide information needed for the auditor to perform his or her audit procedures;

a. 管理层的重大延迟、公司员工不可及、或者管理层不愿提供审计师实施其审计程序所需的资料；

b. An unreasonably brief time within which to complete the audit;

b. 在不合理的时间内完成审计；

c. Unexpected extensive effort required by the auditor to obtain sufficient appropriate audit evidence;

c. 需要审计师付出未曾预料到的巨大努力取得充分适当的审计证据；

d. Unreasonable management restrictions encountered by the auditor on the conduct of the audit; and

d. 审计师在执行审计时遭遇不合理的管理层限制；和

e. Management's unwillingness to make or extend its assessment of the company's ability to continue as a going concern when requested by the auditor.

e. 管理层不愿在审计师要求时就公司的持续经营能力作出或提交其评估。

Note: Difficulties encountered by the auditor during the audit could represent a scope limitation, [39] which may result in the auditor modifying the auditor's opinion or withdrawing from the engagement.

注：审计师在执行审计时遭遇的困难可能表示范围受限，可以导致审计师修改其审计意见或者退出该业务。

Other Matters
其他事项

24. The auditor should communicate to the audit committee other matters arising from the audit that are significant to the oversight of the company's financial reporting process. This communication includes, among other matters, complaints or concerns regarding accounting or auditing matters that have come to the auditor's attention during the audit and the results of the auditor's procedures regarding such matters. [40]

24. 审计师应当向审计委员会传达审计中出现的对于公司的财务报告过程监督而言重大的其他事项。该通报包括审计中引起审计师注意的对于会计或审计事项的抱怨或关切，以及针对这些事项的审计程序的结果。

Form and Documentation of Communications
通报的形式和文档

25. The auditor should communicate to the

25. 审计师应当口头或书

audit committee the matters in this standard, either orally or in writing, [41] unless otherwise specified in this standard. The auditor must document the communications in the work papers, whether such communications took place orally or in writing. [42]

面向审计委员会通报本准则的事项，除非本准则另有要求。审计师必须在工作底稿中存档这些通报，而不论这些通报是口头或书面的。

Note: If, as part of its communications to the audit committee, management communicated some or all of the matters identified in paragraphs 12 or 18 and, as a result, the auditor did not communicate these matters at the same level of detail as management, the auditor must include a copy of or a summary of management's communications provided to the audit committee in the audit documentation.

注：如果审计师由于管理层将第 12 或 18 款指出的某些或所有事项作为其向审计委员会通报的一部分进行过通报，而没有以同样详细的程度通报这些事项，则必须在审计文档中包括一份提交审计委员会的管理层通报或其摘要。

Timing

时　间

26. All audit committee communications required by this standard should be made in a timely manner and prior to the issuance of the auditor's report. [43] The appropriate timing of a particular communication to the audit committee depends on factors such as the significance of the matters to be communicated and corrective or follow - up action needed,

26. 本准则规定的所有审计委员会通报应当及时并且先于审计报告的发布。某个特定的审计委员会通报的适当时间取决于诸如被通报事项的重大性和所需的纠正性或跟进性行动等因素，除非 PCAOB 规

unless other timing requirements are specified by PCAOB rules or standards or the securities laws.

则、准则或证券法律另有规定。

Note: An auditor may communicate to only the audit committee chair if done in order to communicate matters in a timely manner during the audit. The auditor, however, should communicate such matters to the audit committee prior to the issuance of the auditor's report.

注：审计师如果为了在审计中及时通报，可以仅向审计委员会主席通报。但是，审计师应当在发布审计报告之前向审计委员会通报这些事项。

---

① Terms defined in Appendix A, Definitions, are set in **boldface type** the first time they appear.

附录 A［定义］定义的用语首次出现时采用**粗体字**。

② For purposes of this standard, an audit is either an audit of internal control over financial reporting that is integrated with an audit of financial statements or an audit of financial statements only.

对于本准则而言，审计要么是与财务报表审计合并执行的财务报告内部控制审计，要么是单独执行的财务报表审计。

③ See e. g., Section 10A (k) of the Securities Exchange Act of 1934 ("Exchange Act"), 15 U. S. C. § 78j - 1 (k); Rule 2 - 07 of Regulation S - X, 17 C. F. R. § 210. 2 - 07; and Rule 10A - 3 under the Exchange Act, 17 C. F. R. § 240. 10A - 3.

④ Absent evidence to the contrary, the auditor may rely on the company's identification of the appropriate party or parties to execute the engagement letter.

除非有相反证据，审计师可以依赖公司指定的适当方面来履行业务约定书。

⑤ In addition to this inquiry, paragraphs 5. f. and 54 - 57 of Auditing Standard No. 12, Identifying and Assessing Risks of Material Misstatement, describe the auditor's inquiries of the audit committee, or equivalent (or its chair) regarding the audit committee's knowledge of the risks of material misstatement, including fraud risks. These inquiries include, among other things, whether the audit committee is aware of tips or complaints regarding the company's financial reporting.

在该询问之外，审计准则第 12 号［识别和评估重大错报风险］第 5. f 和 54 至 57 款描述了审计师对审计委员会或类似方面（或者其主席）关于审计委员会对于包括舞弊风险在内的重大错报风险的了解的询问。这些询问包括审计委员会是否知悉有关公司财务报表的举报或投诉。

⑥ See AU sec. 317, Illegal Acts by Clients, for a description of the auditor's responsibilities when a possible illegal act is detected. For audits of issuers, see also Section 10A (b) of the Exchange Act, 15 U. S. C. § 78j – 1 (b), and Rule 10A – 1 under the Exchange Act, 17 C. F. R. § 240. 10A – 1.
对于审计师在可能的非法行动被发现时的责任，参见过渡审计准则第 317 条［客户的非法活动］。对于上市公司的审计，还可参见 Section 10A (b) of the Exchange Act, 15 U. S. C. § 78j – 1 (b), and Rule 10A – 1 under the Exchange Act, 17 C. F. R. § 240. 10A – 1。

⑦ See paragraphs 8 – 9 of Auditing Standard No. 9, Audit Planning, for a description of the auditor's responsibilities for establishing an overall audit strategy.
对于审计师制定总体审计策略的责任的描述，参见审计准则第 9 号［审计计划］第 8 至 9 款。

⑧ Auditing Standard No. 12 requires the auditor to determine whether identified and assessed risks are significant risks. A significant risk is defined as a risk of material misstatement that requires special audit consideration.
审计准则第 12 号要求审计师确定已识别和已评定的风险是否重大风险。重大风险是需要特殊审计关注的重大错报风险。

⑨ See paragraph 16 of Auditing Standard No. 9 for the requirement for the auditor to determine whether specialized skill or knowledge is needed to perform appropriate risk assessments, plan or perform audit procedures, or evaluate audit results.
对于审计师确定是否需要特殊技能或知识实施适当的风险评估、计划或实施审计程序或者评价审计结果的要求，参见审计准则第 9 号第 16 款。

⑩ See AU sec. 322, The auditor's Consideration of the Internal Audit Function in an Audit of Financial Statements, which describes the auditor's responsibilities related to the work of internal auditors.
参见过渡审计准则第 322 条［在财务报表审计中审计师对于内部审计部门的考虑］，它描述了审计师与内部审计师的工作有关的责任。

⑪ See paragraphs 16 – 19 of Auditing Standard No. 5, An Audit of Internal Control Over Financial Reporting That Is Integrated with An Audit of Financial Statements, which describe the auditor's responsibilities related to using the work of others in an audit of internal control over financial reporting.
参见审计准则第 5 号［与财务报表审计合并执行的财务报告内部控制审计］第 16 至 19 款，它描述了审计师在财务报告内部控制审计中利用他人工作的责任。

⑫ See paragraphs 8 – 14 of Auditing Standard No. 9, which discuss the auditor's responsibilities for determining the audit strategy, audit plan, and extent to which audit procedures should be performed at selected locations or business units involving multi – location engagements.
参见审计准则第 9 号第 8 至 14 款，它讨论审计师对于确定审计策略、审计计划以及在涉及多场所业务中在选定场所或业务单元实施审计程序的范围等方面的责任。

⑬ See AU sec. 543, Part of Audit Performed by Other Independent Auditors, which discusses the professional judgments the auditor makes in deciding whether the auditor may serve as principal auditor.

参见过渡审计准则第 543 条［部分审计由其他独立审计师实施］，它讨论审计师在决定其是否可以担任主责审计师时所做的职业判断。

⑭ See paragraph 15 of Auditing Standard No. 9, which discusses changes in audit strategy and the audit plan during the course of the audit.

参见审计准则第 9 号第 15 款，它讨论审计过程中审计策略和审计计划的变更。

⑮ See, e. g., Financial Accounting Standards Board Accounting Standards Codification, Topic 235, Notes to Financial Statements, paragraph 235 – 10 – 50 – 1, which requires the entity to disclose a description of all significant accounting policies as an integral part of the financial statements, and paragraph 235 – 10 – 50 – 3, which describes what should be disclosed.

参见美国财务会计准则委员会"会计准则汇编"第 235 章［财务报表附注］第 235 – 10 – 50 – 1 款，它要求该实体披露所有重大会计政策的描述，作为财务报表不可分割的一部分，和第 235 – 10 – 50 – 3 款，它描述应当披露什么。

⑯ See also Section 10A（k）of the Exchange Act, 15 U. S. C. § 78j – 1（k）, and Rule 2 – 07（a）（1）of Regulation S – X, 17 C. F. R. § 210. 2 – 07（a）（1）.

⑰ See AU sec. 342, Auditing Accounting Estimates, which discusses the auditor's responsibilities to obtain and evaluate sufficient appropriate audit evidence to support significant accounting estimates in an audit of financial statements.

参见过渡审计准则第 342 条［审计会计估计］，它讨论审计师在财务报表审计中获取和评价充分适当的审计证据从而支持重大会计估计的责任。

⑱ Id.

⑲ Id.

⑳ See paragraph 71. g. of Auditing Standard No. 12.

参见审计准则第 12 号第 71. g. 款。

㉑ See paragraphs 24 – 27 of Auditing Standard No. 14, Evaluating Audit Results, which describe the auditor's responsibilities related to evaluating the qualitative aspects of the company's accounting practices.

参见审计准则第 14 号［评价审计结果］第 24 至 27 款，它描述审计师在评价公司会计实务的质量方面的责任。

㉒ See paragraph 27 of Auditing Standard No. 14.

参见审计准则第 14 号第 27 款。

㉓ See AU sec. 342, which discusses the auditor's responsibilities to obtain and evaluate sufficient appropriate audit evidence to support significant accounting estimates in an audit of financial statements.

参见过渡审计准则第 342 条，它讨论审计师在财务报表审计中获取和评价充分适当的审计证据从而支持重大会计估计的责任。

㉔ See paragraph .66 of AU sec. 316, Consideration of Fraud in a Financial Statement Audit.

参见过渡审计准则第 316 条［在财务报表审计中对于舞弊的考虑］第 .66 款。

㉕ See paragraphs 30 – 31 of Auditing Standard No. 14, which describe the auditor's responsibilities related to the evaluation of whether the financial statements are presented fairly, in all material respects, in conformity with the applicable financial reporting framework. Other PCAOB standards, such as AU sec. 334, Related Parties, and AU sec. 341, The auditor's Consideration of an Entity's Ability to Continue as a Going Concern, describe the auditor's responsibilities related to evaluation of specific disclosures in financial statements.

参见审计准则第 14 号第 30 至 31 款，它描述审计师评价财务报表是否在所有重大方面遵循适用的财务报告框架公允列报的责任。其他 PCAOB 准则，诸如过渡审计准则第 334 条［关联方］和过渡审计准则第 341 条［审计师对于实体的持续经营能力的考虑］，描述审计师评价财务报表特定披露的责任。

㉖ See also Section 10A（k）of the Exchange Act, 15 U. S. C. § 78j – 1（k）, and Rule 2 – 07（a）（2）of Regulation S – X, 17 C. F. R. § 210. 2 – 07（a）（2）.

㉗ See, e. g. , AU sec. 550, Other Information in Documents Containing Audited Financial Statements. In addition to AU sec. 550, discussion of the auditor's consideration of other information is included in AU sec. 558, Required Supplementary Information, and AU sec. 711, Filings Under Federal Securities Statutes.

参见过渡审计准则第 550 条［包含在经审计财务报表文件中的其他资料］。另外，过渡审计准则第 558 条［规定的其他资料］和过渡审计准则第 711 条［按照联邦证券法律申报］包括了审计师对于其他资料的考虑的讨论。

㉘ See AU sec. 341 for the requirements regarding an auditor's responsibility to evaluate whether there is substantial doubt about a company's ability to continue as a going concern for a reasonable period of time, not to exceed one year beyond the date of the financial statements being audited. Additionally, AU secs. 341. 03a – c provide the auditor with an overview of the requirements for evaluating whether there is substantial doubt about the company's ability to continue as a going concern for a reasonable period of time.

对于审计师评价对于公司在不超过被审计财务报表一年的合理期间持续经营能力是否存在严重疑问的责任参见过渡审计准则第 341 条。另外，过渡审计准则第 341. 03a 至 c 条为审计师提供了评价对于公司在合理期间持续经营能力是否存在严重疑问的要求的概览。

㉙ See AU sec. 341. 06, which provides examples of such conditions and events and AU sec. 341. 07, which discusses the auditor's procedures if the auditor believes there is substantial doubt about the company's ability to continue as a going concern for a reasonable period of time.

参见过渡审计准则第 341. 06 条，它提供了这些状况和事件的举例，以及过渡审计准则第 341. 07 条，它讨论如果审计师相信公司在合理期间持续经营能力存在严重疑问时采取的审计程序。

㉚ See AU sec. 341.08, which discusses the auditor's responsibilities related to the auditor's evaluation of management's plans.

过渡审计准则第 341.08 条，它讨论审计师评价管理层计划的责任。

㉛ See AU sec. 341.12, which describes the effects on the auditor's report. See also AU sec. 341.03c, which discusses the auditor's evaluation of factors that indicate there is substantial doubt about the company's ability to continue as a going concern.

过渡审计准则第 341.12 条，它描述审计报告的影响。另参见过渡审计准则第 341.03 条，它讨论表明公司持续经营能力存在严重疑问的因素的评价。

㉜ See AU sec. 341.10, which discusses the possible effects on the financial statements and the adequacy of the related disclosure.

过渡审计准则第 341.10 条，它讨论对于财务报表的可能影响和相关披露的充分性。

㉝ See AU secs. 341.12 –.16, which discuss the auditor's consideration of the effects on the auditor's report when the auditor concludes that substantial doubt exists about the company's ability to continue as a going concern for a reasonable period of time.

过渡审计准则第 341.12 至 16 条，它讨论当审计师认定公司在合理期间持续经营能力存在严重疑问时对于审计报告的影响的考虑。

㉞ Footnote 13 to paragraph 20 of Auditing Standard No. 14 indicates that misstatements include omission and presentation of inaccurate or incomplete disclosures.

审计准则第 14 号第 20 款的脚注指出错报包括遗漏和不准确或不完整披露的列报。

㉟ See Section 13 (i) of the Exchange Act, 15 U.S.C. § 78m (i), which states, in part, that financial statements prepared in accordance with generally accepted accounting principles and filed with the Securities and Exchange Commission "shall reflect all material correcting adjustments that have been identified by a registered public accounting firm …"

参见《1934 年美国证券交易法》第 13（i）条（15 U.S.C. § 78m（i）），它指出遵循公认会计准则编制并向美国证券交易委员会申报的财务报表"应当反映在册会计师事务所已识别的所有重大纠正性调整……"。

㊱ Appendix B of Auditing Standard No. 14 discusses the qualitative factors related to the evaluation of the materiality of uncorrected misstatements.

审计准则第 14 号附录 B 讨论与未纠正错报的评价有关的质量因素。

㊲ See paragraph 10 of Auditing Standard No. 14, which requires the auditor to accumulate misstatements identified during the audit, other than those that are clearly trivial.

参见审计准则第 14 号第 10 款，它要求审计师累计在审计中识别的错报，除非是明显的小差错。

㊳ See also Section 10A (k) of the Exchange Act, 15 U.S.C. § 78j–1 (k) and Rule 2–07 (a) (3) of Regulation S–X, 17 C.F.R. § 210.2–07 (a) (3).

㊴ See paragraphs .22 –.32 of AU sec. 508, Reports on Audited Financial Statements, for a discussion

of scope limitations.
对于范围限制参见过渡审计准则第 508 条［报告经审计财务报表］。

⑩ AU secs. 316. 79 – . 81 and AU sec. 317. 17 include specific communication requirements relating to fraud or illegal acts, respectively.
过渡审计准则第 316. 79 至 . 81 条和过渡审计准则第 317. 17 条包括与舞弊或非法行为分别有关的具体通报要求。

⑪ See paragraphs . 07 – . 11 of AU sec. 532, Restricting the Use of an auditor's Report, which apply to certain written reports on matters coming to the auditor's attention during the course of the audit.
过渡审计准则第 532 条［限制审计报告的使用］第 . 07 至 . 11 款，它适用于对审计中引起审计师注意的事项的某些书面报告。

⑫ Consistent with the requirements of Auditing Standard No. 3, Audit Documentation, the audit documentation should be in sufficient detail to enable an experienced auditor, having no previous connection with the engagement, to understand the communications made to comply with the provisions of this standard.
与审计准则第 3 号［审计文档］的要求一致，审计文档应当充分详细，使得原先与该业务无关的熟练的审计师能够了解按照本准则的要求做出的通报。

⑬ Consistent with Rule 2 – 07 of Regulation S – X, 17 C. F. R. § 210. 2 – 07, in the case of a registered investment company, audit committee communication should occur annually, and if the annual communication is not within 90 days prior to the filing of the auditor's report, the auditor should provide an update in the 90 – day period prior to the filing of the auditor's report, of any changes to the previously reported information.
与 Rule 2 – 07 of Regulation S – X, 17 C. F. R. § 210. 2 – 07 一致，对于在册投资公司，审计委员会通报应当每年做，并且，如果年度通报不是在审计报告申报之前 90 天之内，审计师应当在审计报告申报之前 90 天之内提交对于原先报告资料的变动。

Appendix A Definitions
附录A - 定义

A1. For purposes of this standard, the terms listed below are defined as follows:

A1. 就本准则而言，以下用语的定义是：

A2. Audit committee — A committee (or equivalent body) established by and among

A2. 审计委员会：公司的董事会为了监督公司的会

the board of directors of a company for the purpose of overseeing the accounting and financial reporting processes of the company and audits of the financial statements of the company; if no such committee exists with respect to the company, the entire board of directors of the company.

计和财务报告过程以及公司的财务报表审计所设立的隶属于董事会的委员会（或同等机构）；如果不存在该委员会，则整个董事会就是审计委员会。

For audits of nonissuers, if no such committee or board of directors (or equivalent body) exists with respect to the company, the person (s) who oversee the accounting and financial reporting processes of the company and audits of the financial statements of the company.

对于非上市公司的审计，如果公司不存在该委员会或董事会（或同等机构），那么，监督公司的会计和财务报告过程以及公司的财务报表审计的人员就是审计委员会。

A3. Critical accounting estimate—An accounting estimate where (a) the nature of the estimate is material due to the levels of subjectivity and judgment necessary to account for highly uncertain matters or the susceptibility of such matters to change and (b) the impact of the estimate on financial condition or operating performance is material.

A3. 关键会计估计：（a）由于主观性程度和核算高度不确定性事项所需的判断或者这些事物的易变性等原因而性质重大的会计估计，和（b）对于财务状况或经营业绩影响重大的会计估计。

A4. Critical accounting policies and practices—A company's accounting policies and practices that are both most important to the portrayal of the company's financial condition and results, and require management's most

A4. 关键会计政策和实务：对于公司财务状况和成果的形象最重要并且需要管理层最困难、主观或复杂判断的会计政策和实

difficult, subjective, or complex judgments, often as a result of the need to make estimates about the effects of matters that are inherently uncertain.

务，通常是由于需要对固有不确定性的事项的影响作出估计。

Appendix B Communications with Audit Committees Required by Other PCAOB Rules and Standards

附录B －其他PCAOB 规则和准则规定的与审计委员会的沟通

This appendix identifies other PCAOB rules and standards related to the audit that require communication of specific matters between the auditor and the audit committee.

本附录列出了要求在审计师和审计委员会之间沟通特定事项的与审计有关的其他 PCAOB 规则和准则。

- Auditing Standard No. 4, Reporting on Whether a Previously Reported Material Weakness Continues to Exist, paragraphs 60, 62, and 64

- 审计准则第 4 号［针对原先报告的实质性弱点是否继续存在进行报告］第 60、62 和 64 款。

- Auditing Standard No. 5, An Audit of Internal Control Over Financial Reporting That Is Integrated with An Audit of Financial Statements, paragraphs 78 – 81, 91, C7, and C14

- 审计准则第 5 号［与财务报表审计合并实施的财务报告内部控制审计］第 78 至 81、91、C7 和 C14 款。

- Auditing Standard No. 12, Identifying and Assessing Risks of Material Misstatement, paragraphs 5. f. and 54 – 57

- 审计准则第 12 号［识别和评估重大错报风险］第 5. f. 款和 54 至 57 款。

• PCAOB Rule 3524, Audit Committee Pre - approval of Certain Tax Services	• PCAOB 规则第 3524 条［特定税务服务的审计委员会预先批准］
• PCAOB Rule 3525, Audit Committee Pre - approval of Non - audit Services Related to Internal Control Over Financial Reporting	• PCAOB 规则第 3525 条［与财务报告内部控制有关的非审计服务的审计委员会预先批准］
• PCAOB Rule 3526, Communication with Audit Committees Concerning Independence	• PCAOB 规则第 3526 条［就独立性与审计委员会沟通］
• AU sec. 316, Consideration of Fraud in a Financial Statement Audit, paragraphs .79 -.81	• 过渡审计准则第 316 条［在财务报表审计中对于舞弊的考虑］第 79 至 81 款。
• AU sec. 317, Illegal Acts by Clients, paragraphs .08, .17, and .20	• 过渡审计准则第 317 条［客户的非法行为］第 08、17 和 20 款。
• AU sec. 325, Communications About Control Deficiencies in an Audit of Financial Statements, paragraphs 4 - 7 and 9	• 过渡审计准则第 325 条［在财务报表审计中就控制缺陷沟通］第 4 至 7 和 9 款。
• AU sec. 328, Auditing Fair Value Measurements and Disclosures, paragraph .50	• 过渡审计准则第 328 条［审计公允价值计量和披露］第 50 款。

- AU sec. 333, Management Representations, paragraph .05

- 过渡审计准则第 333 条［管理层声明］第 05 款。

- AU sec. 550, Other Information in Documents Containing Audited Financial Statements, paragraphs .04 and .06

- 过渡审计准则第 550 条［包含在经审计财务报表文件中的其他资料］第 04 和 06 款。

- AU sec. 711, Filings Under Federal Securities Statutes, paragraph .13

- 过渡审计准则第 711 条［按照联邦证券法律申报］第 13 款。

- AU sec. 722, Interim Financial Information, paragraphs .08 –.09, .30 –.31, and .33 –.36

- 过渡审计准则第 722 条［中期财务资料］第 08 至 09、30 至 31 和 33 至 36 款

Appendix C Matters Included in the Audit Engagement Letter

附录C －审计业务约定书包括的事项

C1. The auditor should include the following matters in the engagement letter. ① The auditor's description of these matters will vary depending on whether the auditor is engaged in a financial statement audit or in an audit of internal control over financial reporting that is integrated with an audit of financial statements ("integrated audit").

C1. 审计师应当在业务约定书中包括以下事项。审计师对于这些事项的描述可能不同，取决于审计师是进行财务报表审计还是进行与财务报表审计合并执行的财务报告内部控制审计（“整合审计”）。

a. The objective of the audit is:

1. Integrated audit: The expression of an opinion on both the effectiveness of internal control over financial reporting and the financial statements.

2. Audit of financial statements: The expression of an opinion on the financial statements.

b. auditor's responsibilities:

1. The auditor is responsible for conducting the audit in accordance with the standards of the Public Company Accounting Oversight Board. Those standards require that the auditor:

(a) Integrated audit: Plan and perform the audit to obtain reasonable assurance about whether the financial statements are free of material misstatement, whether caused by error or fraud, and whether effective internal control over financial reporting was maintained in all material respects. Accordingly, there is some risk that a material misstatement of the financial statements or a material weakness in internal control over financial reporting would remain undetected. Although

a. 审计的目标是:

1. 整合审计:对于财务报表内部控制的有效性和财务报表同时发表意见。

2. 财务报表审计:对财务报表发表意见。

b. 审计师责任:

1. 审计师负责遵照公众公司会计监督委员会的准则执行其审计。这些准则要求审计师:

(a) 整合审计:计划和实施审计,获取关于财务报表是否没有错误或舞弊造成的重大错报以及财务报告内部控制是否在所有重大方面被保持的合理保证。因此,财务报表的某个重大错报或财务报告内部控制的某个实质性弱点仍未被发现是有可能的。尽管不是绝对保证,合理

not absolute assurance, reasonable assurance is a high level of assurance. Also, an integrated audit is not designed to detect error or fraud that is immaterial to the financial statements or deficiencies in internal control over financial reporting that, individually or in combination, are less severe than a material weakness. If, for any reason, the auditor is unable to complete the audit or is unable to form or has not formed an opinion, he or she may decline to express an opinion or decline to issue a report as a result of the engagement.

保证仍然是高水平的保证。而且，整合审计不是被设计成发现不重要的财务报表的错误或舞弊以及个别或合计低于实质性弱点的财务报告内部控制缺陷。无论任何原因，只要审计师不能完成审计或者不能形成或没有形成审计意见，审计师可以拒绝发表审计意见或者拒绝发布作为业务结果的审计报告。

(b) Audit of financial statements: Plan and perform the audit to obtain reasonable assurance about whether the financial statements are free of material misstatement, whether caused by error or fraud. Accordingly, there is some risk that a material misstatement would remain undetected. Although not absolute assurance, reasonable assurance is a high level of assurance. Also, a financial statement audit is not designed to detect error or fraud that is immaterial to the financial statements. If, for any reason, the auditor is unable to complete the audit or is unable to form or has not formed an opinion, he or she may decline to express an opinion or decline to issue a report as a result of the engage-

(b) 财务报表审计：计划和实施审计，获取关于财务报表是否没有差错或舞弊造成的重大错报的合理保证。因此，财务报表的某个重大错报仍未被发现是有可能的。尽管不是绝对保证，合理保证仍然是高水平的保证。另外，财务报表审计不是设计成发现对于财务报表而言不重大的错误或舞弊。无论任何原因，只要审计师不能完成审计或者不能形成或没有形成审计意见，审计师可以拒绝表达审计意

ment.

见或者拒绝发布作为业务结果的审计报告。

2. An audit includes:

2. 审计包括:

(a) Integrated audit: In fulfillment of the responsibilities noted above, the auditor communicates:

(a) 整合审计: 为了履行上述责任,审计师:

(1) To the audit committee and management: all material weaknesses in internal control over financial reporting identified during the audit, in writing.

(1) 向审计委员会和管理层书面通报在审计中识别的所有财务报告内部控制实质性弱点。

(2) To the audit committee: all significant deficiencies identified during the audit, in writing, and informs the audit committee when the auditor has informed management of all internal control deficiencies.

(2) 当审计师已经告知管理层所有内部控制缺陷时,向审计委员会书面通报在审计中识别的所有重大缺陷。

(3) To management: all internal control deficiencies identified during the audit and not previously communicated in writing by the auditor or by others, including internal auditors or others within the company.

(3) 向管理层书面通报原先没有通报的在审计中被审计师或他人(包括公司的内部审计师或其他人员)识别的所有内部控制缺陷。

(4) To the board of directors: any conclusion that the audit committee's oversight of the company's external financial reporting

(4) 向董事会书面通报审计委员会对于外部财务报告和财务报告内部控制

and internal control over financial reporting is ineffective, in writing.

的监督是失效的结论。

(b) Audit of financial statements: Obtaining an understanding of internal control sufficient to plan the audit and to determine the nature, timing, and extent of audit procedures to be performed. ② An audit of financial statements is not designed to provide assurance on internal control or to identify internal control deficiencies. However, the auditor is responsible for communicating:

（b）财务报表审计：了解内部控制，使其足以计划审计和确定将要实施的审计程序的性质、时间和范围。财务报表审计不是设计成提供内部控制的保证或者识别内部控制缺陷。但是，审计师有责任：

(1) To the audit committee and management: all significant deficiencies and material weaknesses identified during the audit, in writing.

（1）向审计委员会和管理层书面通报审计中识别的所有重大缺陷和实质性弱点。

(2) To the board of directors: if the auditor becomes aware that the oversight of the company's external financial reporting and internal control over financial reporting by the audit committee is ineffective, that conclusion, in writing.

（2）如果审计师知悉审计委员会对于外部财务报告和财务报告内部控制的监督是失效的，那么，向董事会书面通报该结论。

c. Management's responsibilities:

c. 管理层责任：

1. Management is responsible for the company's financial statements, including disclosures.

1. 管理层对公司的包括披露在内的财务报表负责。

2. Management is responsible for establishing and maintaining effective internal control over financial reporting.

2. 管理层对于建立和保持有效的财务报告内部控制负责。

3. Management is responsible for identifying and ensuring that the company complies with the laws and regulations applicable to its activities.

3. 管理层对于识别和确保公司遵守适用其活动的法律和法规负责。

4. Management is responsible for making all financial records and relevant information available to the auditor.

4. 管理层对于向审计师提供所有财务记录和相关资料负责。

5. At the conclusion of the engagement, management will provide the auditor with a letter that confirms certain representations made during the audit.

5. 在业务完成阶段，管理层要向审计师提供书面证明，确认在审计中的某些声明。

6. Management is responsible for adjusting the financial statements to correct material misstatements relating to accounts or disclosures and for affirming to the auditor in the representation letter that the effects of any uncorrected misstatements aggregated by the auditor are immaterial, both individually and in the aggregate, to the financial statements taken as a whole.

6. 管理层负责调整财务报表，纠正与账户和披露有关的重大错报，并且在管理层声明中向审计师确认由审计师合计的未纠正错报，无论单独或合计，对于财务报表总体而言是不重大的。

C2. In connection with a review of interim financial information, to confirm and docu-

C2. 审计师为了确认并记录与中期财务资料审阅有

ment the understanding, the auditor should either: (a) document in the audit engagement letter the nature and objectives of the engagement to review interim financial information and the responsibilities of management and the auditor or (b) issue a separate engagement letter that addresses such matters. ③

关的谅解，应当（a）在审计业务约定书中记载中期财务资料审阅业务的性质和目标，以及管理层和审计师的责任，或者（b）签署一份单独的业务约定书处理这些事项。

① Certain matters should not be included in an engagement letter; for example, under Securities and Exchange Commission, Section 602. 02. f. i. of the Codification of Financial Reporting Policies, indemnification provisions are not permissible for audits of issuers.

某些事项不应当包括在业务约定书中；例如，根据美国证券交易委员会《财务报告政策汇编》第 602. 02. f. i 条，不允许为上市公司提供赔偿条款。

② AU sec. 325, Communications About Control Deficiencies in an Audit of Financial Statements, provides direction on control deficiencies identified in an audit of financial statements.

过渡审计准则第 325 条［在财务报表审计中就控制缺陷沟通］对于在财务报表审计中识别的控制缺陷提供指引。

③ Paragraphs .08 –.09 of AU sec. 722, Interim Financial Information, discuss the auditor's responsibilities related to establishing an understanding with the audit committee in connection with a review of the company's interim financial information.

过渡审计准则第 722 条［中期财务资料］第 08 至 09 款讨论审计师在公司中期财务资料审阅中与审计委员会达成谅解的责任。